THE BEST OF CHINESE COOKING

THE BEST OF
CHINESE
COOKING

Bay Books

Published by Bay Books
61–69 Anzac Parade,
Kensington
NSW 2033 Australia

© Bay Books

National Library of Australia
Card Number and ISBN
0 85835 721 6
Photography by Ashley
Barber
Printed in Singapore by
Toppan Printing Co. (S) Pte.
Ltd.

The publishers gratefully
acknowledge the assistance
of the following organisations
in the preparation of this
book: The Home Science
Department of East Sydney
Technical College
(specifically the second year
students of the Home
Economics Certificate Course
who prepared the dishes for
photography, under the
supervision of Anne Kilgour
and Jane Aspinwall); David
Jones Pty Ltd, Sydney;
Josiah Wedgwood & Sons
(Australia); Magnolia's
Emporium, Sydney; Fred
Pazotti Pty Ltd, Sydney; The
Burlington Centre, Sydney;
Slatecraft Pty Ltd, Sydney.

BBR88

Contents

Introduction

The Best of Chinese Cooking contains a wide selection of recipes from various regions of China. These have been arranged into ten chapters, each introduced with general advice on the background and preparation of different types of dishes. Three preliminary sections ('Chinese Cooking Utensils', 'Common Ingredients in Chinese Cooking' and 'Some Useful Techniques') provide useful information on preparing and cooking Chinese food.

Chinese cooking is one of the most highly-regarded cuisines of the world. In China cooking and eating are so inextricably entwined that together they become not only an art but also a recreation and a social activity for the Chinese people.

China has always been dependent on the results of each year's crops to fend off the threat of starvation. To guard against natural disasters, the Chinese people developed techniques very early in their history for preserving and storing food.

The first method of preserving fish, vegetables and fruit was by drying these foods in the sun and the air. Later it was discovered that many foods could be preserved by packing them in salt. Gradually fresh and dried ingredients began to appear in the same dish, producing sophisticated contrasts of flavours as well as stretching a small quantity of a fresh ingredient to feed a large number of people.

Because the quality of the soil is so poor in many regions of China, part of the inventiveness of the cooking can be attributed to necessity as much as to choice. The Chinese discovered that they could use many apparently unappetizing ingredients such as roots and bulbs, fungi, seaweed, marine fauna and even flowers, as well as many other naturally growing foods to provide the interesting variety of tastes in Chinese cooking.

Rice and noodles are the staples of the Chinese diet. It is rare for the accent to be placed on one specific dish and usually the dishes are all served together. Soup is not necessarily considered as the first course, but may be served at any time during the meal or even to conclude the dinner.

In China, all the food is cut into even-sized pieces by the cook so that it cooks evenly and can be lifted easily from the bowl with chopsticks. Vegetables play a more important role than meat. Milk and milk products, including butter, are almost completely absent. Vegetable oils, particularly peanut oil, are used as the principal cooking agents, although lard is used occasionally. Wine is used extensively in Chinese cooking; however dry sherry is a very good substitute.

Regional Cooking

The important difference between dishes of the north and south of China lies in the staple foods. In the south, rice is the staple food, whereas in the north, rice is generally replaced with grain products like noodles and steamed bread. There are four areas which have made distinctive contributions to the national Chinese cuisine: Canton, Peking, Szechuan and Fukien.

Canton and the Southeast

Canton is the region of China that first came in contact with the West. The Chinese from the Canton region were also the first to leave China and introduce their techniques of stir frying and steaming to the world.

Seafood plays an important part in the cooking of southern China. Lobster and crab cooked with ginger and onion is a favourite combination, as is meat with seafood (shown by the popularity of the Cantonese dish, Beef with Oyster Sauce).

Stir frying of vegetables is one of the traditional cooking methods of the southeast, and many cooks are now using this technique in Western kitchens in the knowledge that this retains the maximum amount of vitamins and minerals.

The Cantonese are responsible for creating the many dishes that make up Yum Cha (literally 'drink tea'), a light meal comprising many delicacies and snacks.

Peking and the North

Peking, situated near the Great Wall, is the old Imperial City of China. The hauté cuisine of China developed in Peking, where chefs competed with one another to present the best dishes for the Emperor. Peking cuisine was introduced to the world when embassies were established in which Peking-trained chefs set up kitchens and cooked for staff and visitors. Grain is grown extensively in the northern part of China. The onion family (onion, garlic and shallots) is popular and widely used in northern cooking. Many foods are steamed or clear simmered, a cooking method in which the foodstuffs retain their natural flavours.

The following dishes are typical of northern Chinese cooking: Peking Duck, Peking Doilies, Tung Po Pork.

Szechuan and the West

The most distinctive aspect of the Szechuan school is the widespread use of Szechuan pepper. Strongly spiced and peppered dishes are typical of this region, and the area surrounding Yunan is famous for its ham.

Fukien and the Northeastern Coast Provinces

Fish and seafood gathered from the great rivers and the sea are the favourites of this area, though the importance of soups is a remarkable culinary characteristic. It is quite common to serve two or more soups at any given meal. Most are clear soups. Superior quality soy sauce and red cooked dishes such as Red Simmered Pork distinguish this area.

◄Preserved Red Ginger

Chinese Cooking Utensils

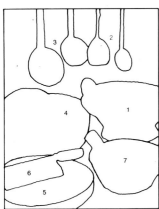

1. Wok
2. Charn (stirring ladle)
3. Strainer
4. Steamer
5. Chopping board
6. Cleaver
7. Clay pot

The equipment shown here is of great use when cooking and preparing Chinese food. The one essential utensil is the wok; substitutes can be found for the others. A wok requires very little maintenance to keep the cooking surface in good condition. Avoid washing the wok in soapy water. Use a wok brush, or similar implement, to wipe away food particles after cooking. Clean the inside of the bowl with a lightly oiled cloth.

Common Ingredients in Chinese Cooking

The following is a selection of ingredients commonly used in Chinese cooking with instructions on how to handle, prepare, use and store. The photograph of widely-used vegetables has been added to assist with identification. Details of preparation and use of these vegetables are included with recipes.

Abalone
A mollusc. Canned abalone is more convenient as it is already cooked and needs only brief reheating. Cooking too long makes it tough. The liquid can be used in soups. Abalone can be kept for a few days in fresh water in the refrigerator. No substitute.

Bamboo Shoots
The young shoots of the bamboo plant are available canned. They need only a very short cooking time. Crisp and with a delicate sweet taste, they can be stored immersed in water and in a covered jar for a few weeks in the refrigerator. Change the water every 3 days. Rinse under cold running water before use.

Bean Curd
Made from soy beans into a sort of milk from which a curd of 'cheese' is obtained. Regarded as a vegetable and an important source of protein, bean curd is very inexpensive and can be combined with almost every other ingredient. May be bought in cakes, in cans or by weight. Bean curd should be handled as little as possible since it is very fragile. It is best kept immersed in water and can be stored only for two to three days at the most.

Bean Sprouts
These are the sprouts of mung peas, the dark green husks of which are often still attached and have to be removed by washing in water and carefully rubbing off.

Remove also any dark and wilted tail ends. The fresh variety is preferable. The crispness can be restored by leaving them in iced water for 30 minutes. They can be kept for a few days by washing them well and storing them in the refrigerator.

Bitter Melon
Also called balsam pear, kareala or bitter gourd, it is the elongated, wrinkled green fruit of a tropical plant; sold in cans and occasionally fresh. Has a distinctive, but not unpleasant, bitter flavour. It is parboiled to remove excess bitterness. Can be kept in the refrigerator in a perforated plastic bag for about five to seven days. Can be substituted by cucumber. Before use, the seedy, spongy, inner part has to be removed.

Celery Cabbage
Also called Chinese lettuce, it is a delicious crisp vegetable with long leaves that are white and firm in the stemlike centre part and light green and fringed at the sides and top. The leaves are tightly rolled together. Ideal for stir-fried dishes. Requires only a short cooking time. Can be kept in a perforated plastic bag in the refrigerator for a few days.

Chillies, Fresh
Care should be taken when handling fresh chillies. Always handle with rubber gloves and prepare under running water. Slit lengthwise with a knife and scrape out the seeds. Use as needed. If chilli juice comes in contact with your eyes, flush immediately with fresh water. Generally, the smaller the chillies, the hotter they are. Substitute dried chillies or chilli sauce, but not chilli pepper.

Chinese Dried Mushrooms
These are dark brown dried mushrooms with rather large caps. They must be soaked in hot water for 20 minutes. Discard the skin and use the cap. They are sold by weight and are rather expensive, but need only be used sparingly. Essential ingredient; no substitute.

Larp Cheong (Chinese sausages)
These Chinese pork sausages have a sweet taste; usually sold in pairs. Can be kept in the refrigerator or freezer for months if wrapped in foil. No substitute.

Five Spice Powder
A brown powdered mixture of star anise, cloves, cinnamon, anise, pepper and fennel. Used sparingly in red-simmered and roasted meat and poultry dishes. Sold loose or in jars. No substitute.

Ginger Root, Fresh
A fibrous, irregularly shaped tubular root of a tropical plant; yellowish ivory coloured inside with a light brown smooth skin. The part which lies directly under the stem is the youngest and

most delicate part as it has very few fibres. Ginger root can be kept alive and even growing, by placing it in a pot covered with earth and sand and regularly giving it water. Take out when needed, slice off what is necessary and return the rest. Ginger root should be lightly scraped, not peeled. It is also possible to keep fresh ginger (washed, scraped and cut into pieces) in sherry in a tightly capped jar in the refrigerator. Never use dried or powdered ginger as a substitute in Chinese cooking. If fresh ginger is not available, use well washed, preserved ginger.

Hoisin Sauce
Comes under many different names. A sweet and spicy, reddish-brown sauce. Used to marinate roast meats or poultry, it is often combined with other sauces as a dip, etc. Made from soy beans. Sold generally in cans or bottles. No substitute.

Lychees
Have a crimson pink skin and translucent, silky white, jelly-like flesh around a big brown seed. Lychees have a very special subtle flavour. Available in cans, occasionally fresh, sometimes dried. Lychees can be used with other fruits as a dessert. Also used sometimes with poultry, prawns and pork.

Rice Noodles
Long, opaque white, brittle threads made of rice flour. Always sold dried. Can be used like egg noodles for cooked and stir-fried dishes. Can also be fried to puff up and become very crisp. This way they are mainly used as a garnish.

Sesame Oil
Oil extracted from sesame seeds, with a very strong, nutty flavour, exclusively used as a flavouring in soups, with stir-fried dishes, etc. It is sold in bottles. Needs no special care in storing. The colour can vary from almost transparent to a dark brown. No substitute.

Soy Sauce
Soy sauce is often referred to as the most important ingredient in Chinese cooking. This brown sauce, made of soy beans and other ingredients, enhances the flavour of almost every dish whether meat, poultry, seafood or vegetables. Two main types are light soy (called Sang Chan) which is more widely used in cooking; and dark soy (to which caramel is added) which

intensifies the taste and colour of a dish. Soy sauces imported from China are the best because they have been matured and aged slowly. They are usually more expensive, but are worth the extra money. No substitute.

Spring Rain Noodles
Made from mung beans and also called vermicelli or rice vermicelli. They are never eaten on their own but are used in soups or with other foods. Soak in warm water for 5 minutes to soften before using. They make a lovely garnish when deep fried for 2 to 3 seconds.

Star Anise
Star-shaped seed cluster containing shiny brown seeds. Not related to the well-known anise seed, but to the magnolia family. Used to flavour red-simmered dishes. Sold by weight. No substitute.

Tangerine Peel
The dried skin of tangerine, a favourite flavouring for duck, but also used with red-simmered dishes, in some soups and sometimes in congee. Only a small piece is used at a time. High prices are paid for tangerine peel that has been left to age for several decades to improve the flavour. Sold by weight. Usually soaked in water for about 20 to 30 minutes. Substitute — a strip of orange rind.

Water Chestnuts
These are squat, dark brown tubers of an aquatic plant that grows in marshes in East Asia. When peeled they are white and crisp with a fresh, sweet taste. Often used together with bamboo in stir-fried dishes. Water chestnuts blend with almost all other ingredients. Available canned. Can be stored immersed in fresh water for about 2 to 3 weeks, in a tightly capped jar. Change the water every 2 or 3 days. No substitute.

Other Leafy Vegetables
There are a number of leafy vegetables available through shops that specialise in Chinese vegetables: Chinese spinach, Chinese broccoli and Chinese cabbage. These and many other fresh vegetables make excellent additions to dishes when used as directed in the recipes.

Chinese vegetables

1. Dried mushrooms
2. White radish
3. Garlic
4. Ginger
5. Shallots
6. Bean sprouts
7. Snow peas
8. Baby corn
9. Coriander
10. Chillies
11. Lotus root
12. Capsicum
13. Tangerine peel.

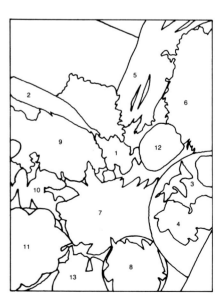

Some Useful Techniques

There are a number of valuable skills to acquire for successful Chinese cooking. Stir frying is a basic technique and deep frying is widely used. Specific skills such as folding wontons, cutting vegetables, sectioning chickens and using chopsticks are all important components of preparing, cooking, presenting and enjoying Chinese food.

Stir Frying

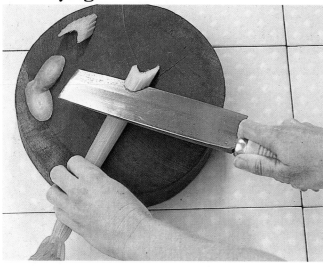

All vegetables must be prepared in advance. Chop, soak or blanch separate ingredients as directed and set aside before cooking starts.

Slice meat into thin strips so that it cooks as quickly as possible. Trim excess fat.

Heat oil in wok until very hot but not sizzling. Fry garlic and ginger first (if they are included in recipe) to flavour oil.

Add onion, tossing and stirring frequently to cook evenly.

Add other vegetables as directed, starting with those that need the longest cooking time. Continue stirring.

Finally add sauce or stock, reduce heat, cover and allow to simmer for a short time until vegetables are tender but still crisp.

Deep Frying

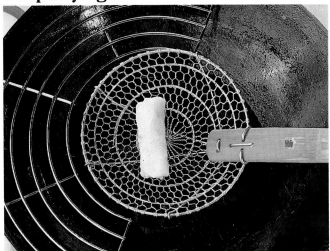 

Heat oil in wok until very hot. Plunge ingredients one at a time into hot oil.

Allow ingredients to fry until crisp and golden all over.

When cooked, place ingredients on a rack to drain and cool.

Using Chopsticks

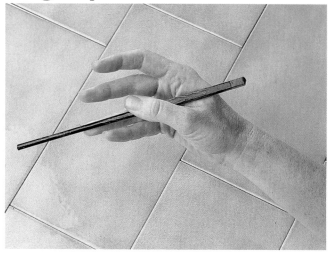

Place one chopstick in the right hand, held by the base of the thumb and the top of the forefinger, fingers slightly bent.

The second chopstick is held by the top of the thumb and the tops of the middle and index fingers.

The first chopstick remains stationary while the second one is moved up and down by the middle and index fingers.

Sectioning Chicken Chinese Style

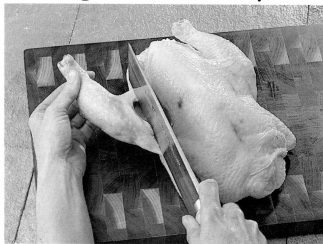

Remove leg and thigh from chicken by cutting lengthwise between thigh and breast.

Halve the chicken by cutting along the backbone from the parson's nose to the neck.

Remove wings and separate drumsticks from thighs at the joints.

Divide wings into two pieces at the joints and chop drumsticks and thighs into three pieces. Slice breasts into three or four pieces depending on the size of the chicken.

Cutting Vegetables Chinese Style

Carrots and celery should be cut diagonally into thin slices.

Peel onion and cut it in half from top to bottom. Slice each half into four wedges. Pull apart wedges into separate pieces of onion.

Wash capsicum, chop in half from top to bottom and remove seeds. Cut each half into three slices, again lengthwise. Chop each slice diagonally to produce diamond shapes.

By cutting each vegetable in a different way, even the simplest Chinese vegetable dish becomes attractive.

Folding Wontons

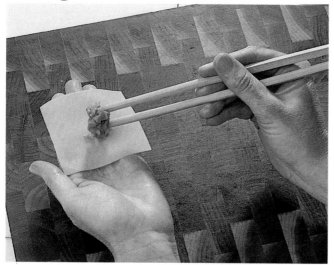

Place a teaspoon of filling in a wonton wrapper.

Fold wrapper diagonally in half and press sides together.

Fold over again, pressing firmly at both sides of the filling but leaving corners open.

Bring two corners together and cross over in front of the filling. Where they meet, brush lightly with water to make them stick.

Open out peak and corners to form crescent shape.

Selection of noodle

RICE AND NOODLES

RICE and noodles are the staple food of the Chinese people. Rice is grown and eaten primarily in the southern part of China. But even apart from the basic necessity of eating rice, to the Chinese the bland taste seems to be the perfect accompaniment to all other foods. When sampling all the myriad taste elements of a Chinese meal, a spoonful of rice taken with the other food as well as in between brings a neutral element into play so that every new morsel can unfold all its full flavour and character.

Long grain rice is suitable for most dishes. When properly cooked, rice absorbs a great deal of water and will be dry and fluffy. Rice is either boiled or steamed. It is very important to wash the rice well to remove the excess starch which otherwise would make the rice too sticky. After it has been boiled or steamed, cooked rice can be fried. It should be completely cooled before it is fried.

Noodles are the food of the North. They are made mainly from grains but sometimes also from seaweed or the starch of mung peas. Noodles are almost always made in thin threads, but there is considerable variety in texture, thickness and width. They can be boiled, steamed, soft fried, deep fried and used in soups.

Chinese Rice

500 g rice
water

Wash rice in cold water until water runs clear. Place rice in saucepan and cover with water to 2.5 cm above rice level. Bring to the boil, reduce heat to medium and continue cooking, uncovered, until water evaporates. (Air bubble holes will form through rice.) When water has evaporated, place lid on saucepan and continue cooking for 7 minutes on low heat. Do not stir or lift lid during last 7 minutes of cooking. If not using immediately, leave in covered pan.

Fried Rice I

1½ cups raw rice
3 eggs
1 tablespoon water
2 tablespoons oil
6 shallots, cut into 1 cm pieces
2 tablespoons soy sauce

Cook rice as described in Chinese Rice recipe. Separate the grains of rice with chopsticks or a fork. Lightly beat the eggs and water.
    Heat the oil in a wok. Add the shallots and stir fry 30 seconds. Add the rice and stir fry until heated through and each grain is coated with oil.
    Pour in the egg mixture and continue stirring until the egg is nearly set. Add soy sauce and stir until well combined. Serve immediately. Serves 4.

Fried Rice II

1½ cups raw rice
2 eggs
1 tablespoon sherry
2 tablespoons oil
12 shallots, cut into 1 cm diagonal pieces
125 g Char Sui, diced (see Char Sui recipe)
½ cup diced smoked ham (optional)
1 tablespoon soy sauce
shallot curls, to garnish

Use chopsticks to separate grains of rice.

Add rice and stir fry.

Pour in egg mixture.

Cook rice as described in Chinese Rice recipe. Separate the grains of rice with chopsticks or a fork. Lightly beat the eggs and sherry.
    Heat the oil in a wok. Add the shallots, roast pork and ham and stir fry 30 seconds. Add the rice and stir fry until heated through and each grain is coated with oil.
    Pour in the egg mixture. Continue stir frying until the egg is nearly set.
    Add soy sauce and stir until well combined. Serve immediately, garnished with shallot curls. Serves 4.

Congee Roast Duck

¾ cup raw rice
6 cups water
2 small dried scallops or 2 tablespoons dried prawns or 1½ teaspoons salt
1 small piece dried tangerine peel
¼ roast duck (wings, legs), cut into bite size pieces
1 tablespoon sherry
2 tablespoons sliced shallots

Place the rice and water in a pan. Add scallops, prawns or salt and tangerine peel. Bring to a boil over high heat. Reduce heat, cover and simmer for 45 minutes.

Add roast duck and sherry. Cover and simmer for at least 1 hour, stirring occasionally and adding some water if the congee becomes too thick.

Remove tangerine peel and dried scallops or dried

prawns, if desired. Top with shallots and serve.
Serves 4.
Note: Substitute a strip of orange rind if no dried tangerine peel is available. Roast duck should be available from speciality Chinese shops, or you may prepare your own. Marinate duck pieces in Char Sui marinade and cook as for Char Sui.

Noodle Cooking

2–2½ litres water
2 teaspoons salt
1 tablespoon oil
500 g noodles

Bring the water, salt and oil to a boil over high heat. Add noodles gradually so that the water maintains the boil.

Boil uncovered 6 minutes for dried noodles and 5 minutes for fresh noodles, stirring occasionally. Test

noodles to see whether they are cooked. If still firm, continue cooking for 1 or 2 more minutes.

Drain noodles and rinse under cold water. If they are to be used right away, drop into boiling water until just

heated through. Drain and use as needed. If to be used later, spread out in a large bowl and sprinkle with a little oil to prevent sticking. Reheat as directed above.
Serves 4 as an accompaniment.

Fried Noodles with Chicken and Vegetables

250 g fresh egg noodles
oil for deep frying
1 whole chicken breast, skinned and boned
250 g green shelled prawns
1 clove garlic, crushed
1 piece bamboo shoot, shredded
6 dried Chinese mushrooms, soaked for 20 minutes in warm water and sliced

125 g vegetables (celery, shallots, beans), cut into matchsticks
½ cup stock
½ teaspoon cornflour
1 tablespoon soy sauce
pinch five-spice powder

Divide noodles into four portions. Deep fry each portion in hot oil until golden brown. Drain on absorbent paper.

Cut chicken meat into strips. Heat wok, add one tablespoon vegetable oil and stir fry chicken and prawns with garlic.

Add bamboo shoots, mushrooms and vegetables and stir fry for further 5

minutes.

Pour in combined mixture of stock, cornflour, soy sauce and five-spice powder and simmer for 5 minutes.

To serve, place noodles on a plate and spoon filling on top. Serve immediately.
Serves 4.

Pork Fried Rice

1½ cups raw rice
3 tablespoons oil
2 eggs, lightly beaten
1 clove garlic, bruised
1 slice fresh green ginger, roughly chopped
6 shallots, cut into 1 cm pieces
250 g Char Sui cut into strips (see Char Sui recipe)
3 tablespoons soy sauce

Cook the rice as described in Chinese Rice. Heat 1 tablespoon oil in wok. Pour in beaten eggs to form a flat omelette; cook for 2 minutes. When bottom is set, flip over and cook for 2 minutes. Remove from heat, roll up (Swiss-roll style) and cut into thin strips. Heat remaining oil in wok, add garlic and ginger and cook until browned; drain and discard. Add shallots and

stir fry for 2–3 minutes. Add stock or water if too dry. Spoon rice into serving dish and garnish with egg strips.
Serves 4.

ried Noodles with Chicken and Vegetables

Steamed Rice and Larp Cheong

1 cup raw rice
1 larp cheong (Chinese
  sausage) cut into 6 mm
  diagonal slices
1 tablespoon sherry
2 dried Chinese
  mushrooms, soaked and
  shredded
coriander

Cook the rice as described in Chinese Rice. Place the larp cheong, sherry and dried mushrooms on top of the rice for the last 7 minutes cooking. Stir the larp cheong and mushrooms through the rice and serve garnished with fresh coriander.

Note: There is no substitute for larp cheong.
Serves 4.

Crispy Noodles

350 g egg noodles
  (preferably fresh)
2 tablespoons oil
1 onion, shredded
½ head celery, shredded
250 g chicken or pork,
  shredded
1 tablespoon soy sauce
oil for deep frying

Separate cooked noodles using chopsticks.

Stir fry vegetables and meat.

Deep fry noodles until crisp.

Cook noodles (as directed in Noodle Cooking). Drain, rinse well and set aside. After about 10 minutes, turn noodles on to a tray and separate them with chopsticks or a fork.

Heat oil in a wok and stir fry vegetables and meat together for about 5–6 minutes. While still crisp, season with a little soy sauce and keep warm.

Put noodles into a strainer, heat the oil for deep frying and plunge strainer into the oil; fry until noodles are crisp then drain on absorbent paper. Turn on to serving dish, add meat and vegetable sauce mixture.
Serves 4.

Crispy Noodles

Noodles in Soup I

3 cups chicken stock
½ Chinese cabbage,
  shredded
60 g Char Sui, shredded
  (see Char Sui recipe)
3 shallots, cut in 2 cm
  pieces

2 tablespoons soy sauce
125 g egg noodles,
  cooked
coriander

Bring stock to boil. Add cabbage and simmer 3 minutes. Add pork and shallots and simmer 1 minute. Stir in soy sauce. Place noodles in individual soup bowls. With a slotted spoon, place some of the pork and vegetables in each bowl. Pour the stock into the bowls and garnish with fresh coriander. Serves 4.

Noodles in Soup II

125 g egg noodles
3 Chinese dried
  mushrooms
125 g lean pork (leg or
  shoulder), sliced
1 tablespoon sherry
1 teaspoon cornflour
2 tablespoons oil
1 thin slice fresh green
  ginger, very finely
  chopped
1 tablespoon soy sauce
3 cups boiling chicken
  stock
4 shallot curls

Cook noodles (as directed in Noodle Cooking) and drain.

Soak mushrooms in warm water for about 20 minutes. Squeeze dry, remove stem and shred caps.

Finely slice the pork across the grain. Mix sherry and cornflour. Add pork and toss to coat.

Heat the oil in a wok, add the ginger and stir fry for 30 seconds. Add the pork and stir fry for 1½ minutes. Add dried mushrooms and stir fry for another 30 seconds.

Add soy sauce to the boiling stock. Place the noodles in individual bowls and pour the stock over the noodles. Top with the pork and mushrooms. Garnish each serving with a shallot curl. Note: If liked, top the soup with a little chilli sauce. Serves 4.

Combination Noodles

500 g egg noodles
1 tablespoon oil
2 dried Chinese
  mushrooms
3 tablespoons oil
1 clove garlic, crushed
1 thin slice fresh green
  ginger, finely chopped
12 shallots, sliced
30 g bamboo shoots,
  shredded
½ chicken breast,
  skinned, boned and cut
  into strips

60 g sliced Char Sui (see
  Char Sui recipe)
90 g bean sprouts
½ cup chicken stock
3 tablespoons soy sauce
1 tablespoon sherry
1 tablespoon cornflour
2 tablespoons water
2 tablespoons Ham
  Garnish

Cook noodles as directed in Noodle Cooking. Rinse under cold running water. Toss with 1 tablespoon oil.

Soak dried mushrooms in hot water for 20 minutes. Squeeze dry, discard stems and cut caps into strips.

Heat the oil in a wok. Add garlic and ginger and stir fry for 30 seconds. Add shallots and stir fry for 30 seconds. Add bamboo shoots and mushrooms and stir fry for 1½ minutes.

Add chicken and pork and stir fry for 5 minutes. Add bean sprouts and stir fry for 20 seconds.

Add chicken stock, soy sauce and sherry. Bring to boil. Blend cornflour and water and add to wok; heat until thickened. Add the noodles, stir lightly and serve immediately. Top with fried mixture and garnish with Ham Garnish (see recipe provided). Serves 4.

Soft Fried Noodles

500 g egg noodles
4 tablespoons oil
6 shallots, sliced
1 tablespoon soy sauce

Cook noodles as directed in Noodle Cooking. Drain, rinse under cold running water, drain and mix with 1 tablespoon oil.

Heat remaining oil in wok until quite hot. Add shallots and stir fry for 30 seconds. Add noodles and stir fry for 2 minutes, separating the noodles with chopsticks.

Add soy sauce and stir fry for another 30 seconds to 1 minute or until completely heated through. Serve plain or combine with a stir fried mixture as indicated in other recipes.
Serves 6.

Soft Fried Rice Noodles

500 g rice noodles
5 tablespoons oil
45 g dried prawns
3 dried Chinese
  mushrooms
½ bunch shallots, cut into
  1 cm pieces
250 g lean pork, cubed
1 tablespoon soy sauce
30 g bamboo shoots,
  shredded
45 g water chestnuts,
  sliced
1 tablespoon chicken
  stock or water
¼ cup preserved tea
  melon or preserved
  sweet cucumber, cubed
coriander leaves (optional)

Cook rice noodles according to packet instructions, drain, rinse under cold running water and mix with one tablespoon oil.

Soak dried prawns and mushrooms separately in warm water for 30 minutes. Drain prawns and squeeze mushrooms dry. Remove mushroom stems and shred caps.

Heat 2 tablespoons oil in a wok. Add shallots and stir fry for about 2 minutes or until it has lost any trace of pink. Add dried prawns and stir fry for a further 30 seconds.

Add soy sauce, bamboo shoots, dried mushrooms and water chestnuts and stir fry for 1½ minutes. Add stock and tea melon and stir fry for another 30 seconds. Remove from pan and keep warm.

Add remaining oil to wok and heat until very hot. Add noodles and stir fry for 1½ minutes or until heated through and very lightly browned. Return meats and vegetables to wok and toss to mix. Place on a serving plate and garnish with coriander if liked.
Serves 6.

Soft Fried Noodles, Pork and Prawns

1 quantity Soft Fried
  Noodles
250 g lean pork
3 tablespoons oil
250 g shelled Royal Red
  prawns
1 tablespoon soy sauce
1 tablespoon sherry
1 clove garlic, crushed
1 slice fresh green ginger,
  finely chopped
1 stalk celery, sliced
  diagonally into 15 mm
  pieces

1 red pepper, seeded and
  cut into 1 cm long pieces
2 tablespoons chicken
  stock or water
Egg Garnish (see recipe
  provided)
shallot curls

Prepare Soft Fried Noodles (see Soft Fried Noodles recipe). Cut pork into slices, across the grain.

Heat 2 tablespoons oil in a wok. Add pork and stir fry for about 2 minutes or until it has lost any trace of pink.

Add prawns and stir fry for 1½ minutes. Add soy sauce and sherry and stir fry for another 30 seconds. Remove pork and prawn mixture from pan.

Add remaining oil and

heat. Add garlic and ginger and stir fry for 30 seconds. Add celery and red pepper and stir fry for 1½ minutes. Add stock and stir fry for 1 minute.

Return pork and prawns to wok and heat through briefly. Add Soft Fried Noodles and toss to mix. Transfer to a serving dish, top with Egg Garnish and garnish with shallot curls.
Serves 6.

Noodles and Meat Sauce

½ bunch shallots
½ cucumber
2 tablespoons Chinese
  brown bean sauce
500 g egg noodles
3 tablespoons oil
1 clove garlic, crushed
1 thin slice fresh green
  ginger, finely chopped
250 g minced pork
¼ cup bamboo shoots
  diced
1 tablespoon sherry
¼ cup beef stock
1 tablespoon each soy and
  hoisin sauce

Diagonally slice half the shallots and set aside; slice the remainder. Peel the cucumber, halve lengthwise and scoop out the seeds; discard. Slice the cucumber and set aside.

Rub brown bean sauce through a sieve.

Cook noodles as directed in Noodle Cooking; drain and mix with 1 tablespoon oil. Keep warm.

Heat remaining oil in wok, add garlic and ginger and stir fry for 30 seconds. Add sliced shallots and stir fry for another 30 seconds. Add pork and stir fry for 1 to 1½

minutes or until it has lost any trace of pink.

Add bamboo shoots and stir fry for another 30 seconds.

Stir in brown bean sauce, sherry, beef stock and soy and hoisin sauce. Reduce heat, cover and simmer for about 4 minutes.

Put noodles in hot bowl and pour the sauce over. Garnish with cucumber and shallots and serve.
Serves 4.

Prawn dipped in sau

STOCKS AND SAUCES

THE Chinese have two main categories of sauces. A number of sauces are incorporated into the dish and have already been mixed with the other ingredients by the cook. The other group of sauces are served on the table as dipping sauces.

The first category includes the famous sweet-sour sauces which are frequently served with deep fried foods. The small amount of sauce which always accompanies stir fried dishes and the meat sauce served on the noodles are also considered to belong to the first category.

Though there are quite a few of these sauces in Chinese cuisine, they are far outnumbered by the sauces and dips used on the table. This last group also includes dry mixes like pepper and salt mix and other condiments, pickles and dressings either packaged or homemade.

Marinades are also widely used in Chinese cooking to flavour and tenderize the food before it is actually cooked.

Chicken Stock

1 × size 15 chicken, quartered
2½ to 3 litres cold water
1 small onion, quartered
½ stalk celery, cut in chunks
3 carrots, peeled and thickly sliced
2 thin slices fresh ginger root
1 tablespoon sherry

Place chicken in a heavy pan. Add cold water and remaining ingredients, bring to a boil and reduce the heat. Cover and simmer 1½ hours. Skim stock during cooking.

Remove chicken from the stock and save for another use.

Strain the stock and chill several hours in the refrigerator. Lift off the fat which will have risen to the surface.

Use as directed in recipes calling for chicken stock. To freeze: Place small amounts of stock in covered containers and freeze until needed.

Meat Stock

1 kg lean pork pieces with bone
3 to 4 chicken wings, necks, back pieces, etc.
2 litres water
1 small onion, quartered
2 carrots, peeled and thickly sliced
2 slices fresh ginger root
2 teaspoons soy sauce

Place pork and chicken pieces in a heavy pan. Add water, onion, carrots and ginger, bring to a boil and simmer for 2 hours. Skim stock during cooking.

Add soy sauce and simmer 5 minutes.

Strain the stock and refrigerate several hours. Lift off the fat which will have risen to the surface.

Use as directed in recipes calling for meat stock. Meat stock may be frozen as indicated in the previous recipe.

Sweet Sour Sauce I

½ cup sugar
½ cup vinegar
2 tablespoons soy sauce
2 tablespoons sherry
3 tablespoons tomato sauce

2 tablespoons cornflour
blended with
½ cup pineapple juice

Combine the sugar, vinegar, soy sauce, sherry and tomato sauce. Bring to boil and add the blended cornflour, stirring constantly until the sauce is thickened. Use as directed in recipes.

Sweet Sour Sauce II

½ cup sugar
½ cup vinegar
4 to 5 tablespoons light soy sauce
1 tablespoon dark soy sauce (optional)
2 tablespoons sherry

1½ tablespoons cornflour
blended with
½ cup water

Combine sugar, vinegar, light soy sauce, dark soy sauce and sherry. Bring to boil and stir in the blended cornflour to thicken. Use as directed in recipes.

Selection of Chinese sauces and seasonings

Sweet Sour Sauce III

½ cup sugar
6 cm thick slice fresh
  green ginger, finely
  chopped
½ cup vinegar
½ cup pineapple juice
1 tablespoon sherry

1½ tablespoons cornflour
blended with
⅓ cup water
125 g Chinese pickle,
  finely sliced

Combine the sugar, ginger,
vinegar, pineapple juice and
sherry. Bring the sauce to boil
and stir in the blended
cornflour to thicken. Stir in
Chinese pickle. Use as
directed in recipes.

Oyster Sauce

If bottled oyster sauce is not available, a fair substitute can be made following this recipe. Do not use smoked oysters or any
other flavoured preparation.

1 × 250 g bottle oysters
1 tablespoon water
1 teaspoon salt
soy sauce
½ tablespoon dark soy
  sauce

Drain oysters and reserve
liquid. Mince the oysters or
chop finely and place in a
saucepan. Add water and
reserved oyster liquid and
bring to boil. Reduce heat,
cover and simmer about 10
minutes.

Remove from heat, add
salt and cool completely.

Force the mixture
through a fine sieve into
saucepan.

Measure the liquid,

adding 2 tablespoons soy
sauce to each ½ cup.

Add dark soy sauce and
bring to boil. Reduce heat and
simmer gently about 7
minutes.

Cool to room
temperature and pour into a
sterilized jar. Seal and store in
the refrigerator. This sauce
can be kept for several weeks.

Plum Sauce

1 cup fresh plums, pitted
  and finely chopped
¼ cup dried apricots,
  soaked in warm water 1
  hour and finely chopped
1 teaspoon chilli sauce
1 teaspoon salt
2 tablespoons water
½ cup sugar
½ cup vinegar

Place the plums and apricots in a heavy wok. Add chilli sauce, salt and 2 tablespoons water. Bring to boil and simmer gently 15 minutes. Add a little more water if the mixture becomes too dry.

Stir in sugar and vinegar and simmer 20 to 30 minutes until the sauce reaches a chutney-like consistency. Place the sauce in a covered sterilized jar and refrigerate when cool. The sauce will keep several months.

Pepper and Salt Mix

3 tablespoons salt
2 tablespoons Szechuan
  peppercorns or crushed
  peppercorns

Heat wok until very hot. Place salt and peppercorns in the pan. Reduce the heat and stir the mixture 5–6 minutes or until the salt is light brown.

Remove from the pan and crush the peppercorns in a mortar and pestle. Sift the mixture through a sieve. Store the pepper and salt mix in a tightly covered jar.

Ginger-Soy Dip Sauce

2 tablespoons oil
1 teaspoon finely chopped
  shallots, white part only
½ teaspoon finely grated
  fresh green ginger
4 tablespoons soy sauce

Heat oil in wok, add shallots and ginger root. Stir fry 20–30 seconds. Add soy sauce. Remove from heat. Serve with white cooked chicken.

Sherry-Soy Dip Sauce

2 tablespoons sherry
2 tablespoons soy sauce
¼ teaspoon sugar

Combine all ingredients and stir together until the sugar has dissolved. Serve as a dip for white cooked or deep fried chicken.

Preserved Red Ginger

250 g fresh ginger,
  skinned and shredded
1 tablespoon salt
2 cups vinegar
1 cup sugar
1 teaspoon red food
  colouring

Sprinkle ginger with salt and stand 2 hours. Rinse thoroughly and drain.

Heat vinegar in wok and stir in the sugar until dissolved. Add ginger, cover and simmer gently for about 10 minutes. Remove from the heat, add food colouring and stir. Let cool completely. Transfer to a sterilised jar, cap and refrigerate.

Preserved red ginger will keep for at least 1 year or longer. Use for garnishing.

SOUPS

THERE is an immense variety of soups in Chinese cooking, some are light and clear and others are thick and filling. They may be either bland and served to clear the palate, or spicy and pungent, served as a contrast with other foods. They range from an inexpensive and simple stock with a few greens or some egg threads added, to very costly and time-consuming preparations, like shark's fin soup.

Most soups have a short cooking time, though some thick and hearty soups, which have dried or salted ingredients added for extra flavour, require a longer time.

Most green vegetables are only added in the last few minutes so they will retain their crispness and bright colour. When tougher vegetables, like carrots are used, they are parboiled first and then added with the more tender leafy vegetables.

The basis of a soup can be water, but more frequently a light, though rich, stock will be used. Soy sauce, ginger juice and sesame oil are often added in small quantities for extra flavour.

Though some soups are eaten to begin the meal, they are also served as a wonderful accompaniment to rice dishes. There are a number of sweet soups in Chinese cooking which are served only at formal dinners or banquets, and these are customarily eaten at the end of a meal.

Garnishes for Soup

Both shredded ham and egg are frequently used to garnish soups and other dishes.

Ham garnish
Cut a thick slice of ham into shreds. The pieces are usually placed in the centre rather than being scattered over the top of the dish.

Egg garnish
Beat one egg until just combined. Heat 1 teaspoon oil in a wok. Add the egg and tilt the wok to form a layer of egg. Cook the egg until set, roll up Swiss roll style, and cut into slices. As with the ham garnish, the strips of egg are placed in the centre of the dish. Both ham and egg garnish may be diced.

Wonton Soup

For the wontons:
16 wonton wrappers
2 dried Chinese mushrooms
90 g lean minced pork
60 g prawns, minced
2 water chestnuts, very finely chopped
4 shallots, very finely chopped
1 tablespoon soy sauce
2 teaspoons sherry
1 egg, lightly beaten

For the soup:
6 cups chicken stock
6 shallots, white part only, thinly sliced
1 quantity Egg Garnish

Soak dried mushrooms in warm water for 20 minutes. Squeeze dry. Remove stalks and finely chop the caps. Combine mushrooms, pork, prawns, water chestnuts, shallots, soy sauce and sherry. Stand 30 minutes. Place ½ teaspoon of filling barely off centre of each wrapper. Fold wrapper in half and press the edges together to seal them. Again, fold the wrapper in half. Pull the corners down into a crescent shape, overlapping the corners. Seal the overlap with a little of the beaten egg.

Drop the wontons one by one into boiling salted water and simmer 7 minutes. (Make sure they do not stick to the bottom of the pan.) Drain the wontons. Bring chicken stock to the boil. Add wontons and shallots. Top each serving with a little of the Egg Garnish.
Serves 6–8.

Place filling in wonton wrapper and fold in half, pressing edges together.

Fold wrapper in half again, opening up overlapping wrapper at each side.

Bring corners together, using egg to fasten overlapping corner tips.

Combination Soup

60 g lean pork, very finely chopped
60 g Royal Red prawns, very finely chopped
2 dried Chinese mushrooms, soaked and shredded
½ teaspoon soy sauce
¼ teaspoon chilli sauce
¼ teaspoon hoisin sauce
1 small egg white
1 litre beef stock
500 g medium size shelled green prawns
extra 4 dried Chinese mushrooms
60 g bamboo shoot, shredded
1 green capsicum, cut into diamonds
1 red capsicum, cut into diamonds
125 g fresh egg noodles, cooked
chilli sauce to serve

Combine the pork, prawns, Chinese mushrooms, soy, chilli and hoisin sauces and egg white. Beat well until thoroughly combined.

Soak the extra dried mushrooms in warm water for 20 minutes, discard the stems and slice the caps.

While the mushrooms are soaking, shape the pork mixture into small rounds.

Bring the stock to the boil and add the pork rounds.

Simmer until nearly cooked then add the prawns. Simmer for a further 3 minutes. Add the remaining ingredients and gently heat through. Serve topped with a spoonful of chilli sauce.

Serves 6.

Sweet Corn and Chicken Soup

1 whole chicken breast
3 cups chicken stock
1 × 220 g can creamed sweet corn
1 tablespoon sherry
1 teaspoon cornflour
blended with
1 tablespoon water
1 egg, beaten
60 g Ham Garnish

Skin and bone the chicken breast then finely chop the meat.

Bring the stock to the boil, skimming if necessary. Reduce the heat, add the chicken and simmer until the meat is cooked.

Add the corn and simmer for a further 5 minutes. Add the blended cornflour and cook over a gentle heat until slightly thickened. Remove from heat.

Stir the soup fairly rapidly to create a 'whirlpool' and pour in the beaten egg in a steady stream.

Serve topped with the Ham Garnish.

Serves 6.
Note: It is most important not to boil this soup as the chicken will become very tough. Always add the egg off the heat and serve the soup hot.

Pork and Abalone Soup

1 × 125 g can abalone
125 g lean pork, trimmed
4 cups chicken stock
2 tablespoons sherry
1 tablespoon soy sauce
2 tablespoons oil
2 thin slices fresh green ginger
1 clove garlic, bruised
45 g bamboo shoots, shredded
fresh coriander

Drain abalone and reserve the liquid. Thinly slice the abalone and pork then cut into 4 cm pieces. Combine abalone liquid, chicken stock, sherry and soy sauce.

Heat chicken stock mixture to boiling point.

Heat the oil in a wok. Add ginger and garlic and stir fry until golden; discard. Add the pork and stir fry until the meat changes colour; drain. Add pork, abalone and bamboo shoot to chicken stock. Cook only to heat through or abalone will toughen. Serve in individual bowls. Float a sprig of coriander in each bowl.

Serves 4.

Crab and Sweet Corn Soup

1.5 litres chicken stock
1 × 220 g can crabmeat, flaked
1 × 125 g can creamed sweet corn
1 tablespoon cornflour
1 tablespoon sherry
2 teaspoons oil
½ teaspoon sesame oil
2 eggs, beaten
2 shallots, finely chopped

Bring stock to the boil in wok. Add crabmeat and corn and simmer for 2 minutes.

Blend cornflour, sherry and oils and add to wok. Bring to the boil; remove from heat.

Immediately pour in beaten egg in a steady stream to form flower patterns on the surface. Sprinkle with chopped shallots and serve.

Serves 6.

Crab and Pork Soup

10 dried Chinese
  mushrooms
1 litre beef stock
250 g lean pork, cut in
  strips
1 × 220 g can crab, flaked
2 tablespoons raw rice
1 onion, very finely
  chopped
1 tablespoon soy sauce
few drops chilli sauce

Cover mushrooms with hot water, stand 20 minutes then drain. Remove stems and discard. Shred caps. Bring stock to boil. Add pork strips and simmer until tender.

Stir in mushrooms, crab meat and rice. Add onion and soy sauce. Simmer until rice is tender. Serve hot, with chilli sauce to taste.
Serves 4.

Pork and Prawn Soup

350 g egg noodles
3 tablespoons oil
1 small onion, thinly sliced
2 slices fresh green
  ginger, finely chopped
250 g lean pork, finely
  shredded
50 g dried Chinese
  mushrooms, soaked and
  shredded
½ Chinese cabbage,
  shredded, blanched
100 g bean sprouts
125 g Royal Red prawns
2 tablespoons soy sauce
4 cups beef or chicken
  stock

Cook the noodles as directed in Rice and Noodles section. Drain.

Heat the oil in a wok. Add onion, ginger and pork and stir fry for 2 minutes.

Add the mushrooms, cabbage, bean sprouts and prawns; stir fry for 2 minutes. Stir in soy and stir fry a

further 1½ minutes. Remove from heat and keep warm.

Bring stock to the boil. Add half the pork mixture and bring to the boil again. Add noodles and heat through. Serve soup and top with remaining hot pork mixture.
Serves 6.

Peking Hot Sour Soup

4 dried Chinese
  mushrooms
4 cups chicken stock
125 g lean pork, shredded
60 g canned bamboo
  shoots, shredded
2 bean curd cakes, cut
  into 1 cm cubes
2 tablespoons white
  vinegar
1 tablespoon soy sauce
1 tablespoon cornflour
4 tablespoons water
1 egg, beaten
½ teaspoon sesame oil
3 shallots, chopped

Soak dried mushrooms in hot water for 20 minutes. Squeeze dry and remove stems. Cut mushroom caps into thin strips.

Bring stock to the boil and add pork and mushrooms. Bring to the boil again, reduce heat and simmer for about 8 to 10 minutes. Add the bamboo shoots and bean curd and simmer for another 4 to 5 minutes.

Mix vinegar and soy sauce and stir into soup. Stir

in blended cornflour and water and simmer, stirring constantly, until thickened.

Stir in the beaten egg off the heat. Add sesame oil and shallots and serve hot.
Serves 4–6.

Chicken Noodle Soup

125 g egg noodles, fresh
  or dried
1 whole chicken breast
1 litre chicken stock
50 g canned bamboo
  shoots, shredded
4 dried Chinese
  mushrooms, soaked and
  shredded
2 tablespoons soy sauce
½ bunch Chinese
  spinach, shredded

Cook the noodles. See Rice and Noodles.

While the noodles are cooking, skin and bone the chicken breast then shred the meat.

Bring the stock to a boil, add the chicken, bamboo shoots, mushrooms and soy and simmer until the chicken is tender. Add the drained noodles and spinach and

gently heat through. Serve hot.
Serves 6.

VEGETABLES

ONE of the most remarkable aspects of Chinese cooking is the approach to vegetables. They are of the utmost importance. This emphasis is due partly to the influence of the Buddhist monks who established strict vegetarian rules. Small wonder this resulted in the development of extraordinary skill in preparing vegetables. To the Chinese, vegetables are not just an accompaniment to meats and other foods, but play an important role of their own. When combined with other ingredients they are at least equally as important as the meats.

The main difference between the Chinese method of cooking vegetables and the Western way is that in the Chinese way, vegetables are cooked only long enough to bring out all their qualities of crispness, tenderness and brightness of colour. The vegetables are served at the peak of their flavour. This does not mean that they are served raw; even in salads, the vegetables will usually be cooked for a brief period of time.

The initial preparation depends largely on how the vegetable will be used. Cutting is of the utmost importance in the preparation of vegetables. Vegetables are cut, blanched and parboiled in such a way that the final cooking can be completed at one time, even though the textures of the individual vegetables differ greatly. The soft leafy vegetables require less cooking than the tougher ones.

Though vegetables may be steamed, braised and even deep fried, stir frying is the favourite cooking technique. Flavourings such as garlic or ginger, are often added to the oil first, the vegetables are stir fried, then soy sauce and sometimes a little sugar is added. Apart from the fact that stir frying will bring out all the fine qualities that appeal to the tastebuds as well as to the eyes, vegetables prepared this way are particularly healthy because there is only a negligible loss in vitamins. After the stir frying, a liquid such as chicken broth is added and the pan is covered.

To ensure their absolute freshness, vegetables should, if possible, be bought on the day they will be served. In China, bean curd is regarded as a vegetable.

Stir Fried Sweet and Sour Vegetables

1 green pepper
1 medium onion
2 sticks celery
2 carrots
2 tablespoons oil
1 clove garlic, crushed
2 thin slices fresh green
  ginger, finely chopped
½ cup shredded canned
  bamboo shoots
3 tablespoons vinegar
2 tablespoons sugar
1 tablespoon sherry
2 tablespoons chicken
  stock
1 tablespoon cornfour
blended with
2 tablespoons water

Remove membrane and seeds from pepper and cut into 5 cm long diamond shapes. Peel the onion, halve lengthwise and cut each half into 1 cm wide strips lengthwise. Cut celery in 5 cm pieces diagonally. Cut carrots in a rolling cut, diagonally into 4 cm pieces. Par-boil 3–4 minutes.

Heat oil in wok, add garlic, ginger and stir for 1 minute. Add the vegetables and stir fry over high heat about 2 minutes. Add vinegar, sugar, sherry and chicken stock and bring to boil. Stir in blended cornflour mixture to thicken.
Serves 4.

Braised Vegetables

2 tablespoons oil
1 teaspoon sesame oil
1 clove garlic, crushed
1 teaspoon fresh green
  ginger, finely chopped
500 g prepared mixed
  vegetables
½ cup hot water
1 tablespoon oyster sauce
1 tablespoon soy sauce
2 teaspoons cornflour
1 tablespoon water

In a wok heat oil and add sesame oil, garlic and ginger. Add vegetables and stir fry 2 minutes. Add hot water, oyster and soy sauces. Simmer 4 minutes.

Push vegetables to one side of wok, add cornflour mixed with water and stir until thick. Fork vegetables through thickened sauce and serve with boiled rice.
Serves 4.

Stir Fried Bean Sprouts

375 g bean sprouts
1 thin slice fresh green
  ginger, finely chopped
½ green pepper, sliced
½ medium sized onion,
  cut into wedges
12 shallots, sliced
2 thin slices ham,
  shredded
2 tablespoons chicken
  stock
combined with
½ tablespoon sherry
2 tablespoons oil

Blanch bean sprouts in
boiling water.

Stir fry vegetables.

Add combined stock and
sherry.

Pour boiling water over bean
sprouts and let stand 20
seconds. Wash in cold
running water, drain and dry.
Arrange the ingredients on a
plate in the order in which
they are to be cooked.
    Heat the oil in a wok.
Add ginger root and stir fry ½
minute. Add green pepper,
onion and shallots and stir fry

1½ minutes. Add bean
sprouts and ham and stir fry
½ minute. Add combined
stock and sherry and bring to
the boil. Remove from the
heat and serve.
Serves 4.

Stir Fried Bean Sprouts

Stir Fried Broccoli and Bean Curd in Oyster Sauce

Stir Fried Broccoli and Bean Curd in Oyster Sauce

500 g broccoli
2 tablespoons oil
fresh green ginger, sliced,
  to taste
1 clove garlic, finely
  chopped
¼ cup canned bamboo
  shoots, shredded
2 cakes bean curds, 1 cm
  cubes
2 tablespoons oyster
  sauce
1 tablespoon soy sauce
½ cup chicken stock
1 teaspoon cornflour
2 tablespoons water

Cut wide broccoli stems in half.

Stir fry ginger to flavour oil.

Add chicken stock and sauces.

Cut off flowerets from broccoli stems. Discard tough ends and cut wide stems in half lengthwise. Then cut in 2 cm pieces diagonally. Par-boil in a large quantity of salted water 3–4 minutes. Drain and rinse broccoli under cold running water. Cool completely.

Heat 2 tablespoons oil in wok until very hot. Add ginger root and garlic. Stir fry for 1 minute until ginger is lightly browned. Discard ginger and garlic. Add the drained broccoli and stir fry for 1 minute. Add bamboo shoots, bean curd, sauces and chicken stock. Bring to boil, reduce heat. Cover wok and simmer for about 2 minutes. Stir in the blended cornflour and water to thicken the sauce. Serves 4.

Vermicelli and Vegetables

4 dried Chinese mushrooms
⅓ cup oil
2 onions, cut into wedges
1 garlic clove, crushed
1 green pepper, sliced
1 red pepper, sliced
3 sticks celery, sliced
250 g bean sprouts
8 canned water chestnuts, halved
¾ cup pineapple juice
1 tablespoon white vinegar
1 teaspoon chilli sauce
1 tablespoon oyster sauce
1½ tablespoons soy sauce
250 g vermicelli noodles, soaked in warm water for 20 minutes and drained

Soak Chinese mushrooms in hot water for 20 minutes, then drain and squeeze. Discard stalks and slice caps.

Heat oil in wok. Add onion, garlic, red and green pepper, celery and stir fry for 3–4 minutes.

Stir in mushrooms, bean sprouts and chestnuts. Pour over pineapple juice, vinegar and sauces. Bring to the boil.

Stir in vermicelli, reduce heat and simmer, stirring occasionally for 3–5 minutes until vermicelli is tender. Serves 4.

Fried Mixed Vegetables

3 tablespoons oil
1 clove garlic, crushed
4 slices fresh green
  ginger, finely chopped
½ Chinese cabbage,
  sliced
1 small green pepper,
  shredded

250 g broccoli, trimmed
  into flowerets
125 g bean sprouts,
  washed and shaken dry
¾ cup chicken stock
2 teaspoons soy sauce
1 teaspoon brown sugar

In a large wok heat oil and add garlic and ginger. Stir fry for one minute. Add cabbage, green pepper and broccoli and stir fry for 3 minutes.

Add the bean sprouts and stir fry for one minute. Stir in stock, soy sauce and sugar. Cook for 3 minutes and serve.
Serves 4.

Stuffed Bean Curd

Cut bean curd cakes in half.

Carefully stuff cakes with filling.

Steam cakes in a shallow dish.

6 cakes bean curd
125 g lean pork, minced
6 shallots, minced
2 water chestnuts, minced
½ tablespoon soy sauce
1 tablespoon sherry
1 egg yolk
1½ tablespoons oil
1 thin slice fresh green
  ginger, finely chopped
1 clove garlic, crushed
1 cup celery, cabbage or
  other seasonal green
  vegetable, cut in to 4 cm
  diamonds
¾ cup chicken stock
2 tablespoons soy sauce
1 tablespoon sherry
1 tablespoon cornflour
2 tablespoons water

Cut the bean curd cakes in half. Make a pocket in each half to contain the filling, taking care not to break the bean curd. In a bowl, mix together the pork, shallots and water chestnuts. Add soy sauce, sherry and egg yolk and mix well. Stuff the bean curd carefully with this mixture.

Place the bean curd on a large shallow heatproof dish and steam for about 25 minutes.

Meanwhile, about 5 minutes before the steaming is completed, heat oil in wok. Add ginger and garlic clove. Stir fry for 1 minute until golden brown. Discard the ginger and garlic. Increase the heat, add the celery or cabbage and stir fry for 1 minute. Add chicken stock, soy sauce and sherry.

Reduce the heat, cover and continue cooking for 1½ minutes. Blend cornflour in water and stir into vegetables. Cook 30 seconds until thickened. Remove dish with bean curd from the steamer. Serve with sauce and Chinese Rice.
Serves 4.

Stuffed Bean Curd

BEEF has historically always been scarce, because cattle themselves are not raised extensively, and the small number of cattle that are found are used to work on the fields. Beef is also prepared in many ways in Chinese cooking.

Round steak, skirt steak, sirloin steak and fillet are the cuts most generally used. Skirt steak is preferred because of its easily recognizable muscular structure. The colour of the beef should be a beautiful red, and all the fat is trimmed away before it is cooked or served.

Mongolian Hot Pot

500 g rump steak
2 onions, cut into wedges
1 bunch shallots, sliced
125 g snow peas, topped and tailed
125 g Chinese cabbage, sliced
125 g bean sprouts
1 red capsicum, cut into wedges
125 g bean curd
125 g egg noodles, cooked
1 quantity meat stock

Remove fat from the meat and slice thinly across the grain. Arrange the meat, vegetables and noodles attractively on a large serving platter.

Heat the firepot at the table, bringing the stock to the boil. Using small wire baskets, guests select and cook own food in boiling stock. At end of meal remaining vegetables, meat and noodles are added to stock and served as a soup. Serves 4.

Gingered Beef

1 teaspoon grated green ginger
1/3 cup soy sauce
2 teaspoons cornflour
500 g rump steak, trimmed and thinly sliced across the grain
4 dried Chinese mushrooms
1/4 cup oil
5 cm piece fresh ginger, peeled and shredded
125 g canned bamboo shoots, drained and cubed

In a large bowl combine grated ginger, soy sauce and cornflour. Add meat and mix well. Allow to marinate for 1 hour, stirring occasionally.

Cover mushrooms with hot water and stand 20 minutes. Drain, remove stems and discard. Slice mushroom caps.

Remove meat from marinade. Heat oil in wok over moderate heat. Add ginger and stir fry for 3 minutes. Add meat, bamboo shoots and mushrooms and stir fry until meat is cooked. Add marinade and heat through.

Serve on a bed of rice or boiled noodles.
Serves 4.

Gingered Beef

Mongolian Hot Pot

Stir Fried Shredded Beef and Celery

500 g rump steak, trimmed
½ bunch celery
2 tablespoons sherry
2 tablespoons soy sauce
½ teaspoon sesame oil
3 teaspoons cornflour
4 tablespoons oil
½ cup chicken stock
2 tablespoons water

Cut the beef across the grain into thin strips. String the celery if necessary, then diagonally slice.

Combine sherry, soy sauce, sesame oil and 2 teaspoons of the cornflour in a bowl. Add the beef and toss to coat. Stand about 10 minutes.

Heat half the oil in a wok. Add beef and stir fry, in two batches, for 3 minutes. Remove beef and keep warm.

Heat remaining oil in the wok, add celery and stir fry for 1 minute. Add chicken stock and simmer for 2 to 2½ minutes. Return beef to wok and heat through. Blend cornflour and water, add to wok and stir until thickened. Serves 4.

Stir Fried Beef with Onions

500 g rump steak, trimmed
3 tablespoons soy sauce
1 tablespoon dry sherry
4 onions
½ cup oil
2.5 cm piece fresh green ginger, peeled and thinly sliced

Slice the beef across the grain then cut into 4 cm pieces. Halve, peel and top and tail the onions. Place the onions, cut side down, on a chopping board and slice each half into 4 wedges. Separate the wedges.

Combine soy sauce and sherry, add to meat mixing thoroughly. Set aside for 10 minutes. Heat half the oil in wok over moderate heat. Add the onions and stir fry for 5 minutes. Remove and set aside. Add remaining oil to wok and heat. Add beef strips and stir fry, in two batches, until the meat changes colour. Return onions and stir fry until heated through. Serve with noodles.
Serves 4.

Braised Beef

3 tablespoons oil
1 kg topside steak, cut into 2 cm cubes
½ cup soy sauce
½ cup sherry
2 cups boiling water
1 small onion, cut into wedges

Heat the oil in a wok. Stir fry the beef cubes until lightly browned. Add soy sauce and bring to boil. Reduce the heat, cover and simmer 8 minutes.

Add sherry and simmer, covered, 5 minutes. Add the remaining ingredients and

bring to boil. Reduce heat, cover and simmer 1 hour or until very tender.
Serves 6.

Szechuan Beef Parcels

3 tablespoons soy sauce
2 tablespoons sherry
1 tablespoon oyster sauce
3 teaspoons sesame oil
500 g rump steak, sliced thinly across the grain
2 cm piece fresh green ginger, peeled and shredded
½ bunch shallots
1 tablespoon hoisin sauce
1 teaspoon chilli sauce
1 tablespoon oil
6 dried Chinese mushrooms, soaked and diced
greaseproof paper
oil for deep frying

Combine the soy sauce, sherry, oyster sauce and sesame oil in a bowl. Stir in the sliced beef, ginger, shallots, hoisin and chilli sauces and oil; marinate for 15 minutes. Add the prepared mushrooms.

Cut out 8 rectangular pieces of greaseproof paper which are large enough to wrap the beef. Divide beef mixture between the pieces of paper and wrap envelope style, tucking in the flaps to secure. Heat the oil for deep frying and fry half the parcels for 2 minutes. Drain well and set aside. Repeat with the remaining beef. Reheat the oil

and refry the beef parcels for a further 1 to 2 minutes. Drain well. Serve garnished with shallot brushes.

Open the parcels with fingers or chopsticks. If opening with fingers, set the table with finger bowls.
Note: Use a good quality greaseproof paper for the beef. Waxed paper is not suitable. If available, Bakewell's Non Stick Baking Parchment is excellent.
Serves 4.

Red Simmered Beef

1 kg piece topside steak
3 tablespoons oil
1 clove garlic, crushed
2 thin slices fresh green
  ginger, finely chopped
½ cup soy sauce
⅓ cup sherry
water to cover
2 whole star anise
1 small piece cinnamon
  stick

Tie the meat at 5 cm intervals so that it will hold its shape while cooking. Heat the oil in wok. Brown the beef on all sides over high heat. Add the remaining ingredients.

Bring the liquid to a boil over high heat. Reduce the heat, cover the wok and simmer for 1½ hours, turning the beef every 30 minutes.

Slice the beef and serve hot or cold with some of the sauce.
Note: The sauce can be refrigerated and kept for use in other dishes. If the sauce is heated to boiling point every few days, it will keep for several weeks.
Serves 6.

Tie beef at 5 cm intervals.

Brown beef on all sides.

Baste with sauce while simmering.

Slice beef and serve hot or cold.

Stir Fried Beef in Oyster Sauce

500 g rump steak, trimmed
2 teaspoons cornflour
1 tablespoon water
2 tablespoons oyster
  sauce
½ cup beef stock
1 tablespoon sherry
1 tablespoon soy sauce
2 tablespoons oil

1 thin slice fresh green
  ginger, finely chopped
1 clove garlic, finely
  chopped
6 shallots, sliced
few sprigs fresh
  coriander

Cut the beef across the grain into strips. Combine the cornflour and water. Combine oyster sauce, stock, sherry and soy sauce.

Heat the oil in a wok. Stir fry the ginger and garlic until lightly browned. Add the beef and stir fry, in batches,

until it has lost any trace of red.

Add the oyster sauce mixture and shallots. Stir fry for 1 to 1½ minutes until hot. Stir in cornflour mixture and heat until thickened. Serve garnished with coriander.
Serves 4.

Beef with Snow Peas

500 g snow peas
3 tablespoons oil
2 teaspoons oyster sauce
500 g rump steak
2 cloves garlic, finely
  chopped
2 thin slices fresh green
  ginger, shredded
1 tablespoon soy sauce
1 red chilli, seeded and
  sliced

Top and tail the snow peas and wipe with a damp cloth if necessary. Heat 1 tablespoon of the oil in a wok, add the snow peas and stir fry for 1 minute. Add the oyster sauce and toss to coat. Remove and keep warm.

Trim the meat and cut into 4 pieces. Heat the remaining oil, add the meat, garlic and ginger and cook until the meat is sealed on both sides. Remove and cut the meat into strips. Return to the wok and continue stir frying for a further 5 minutes. Sprinkle with the soy.

Remove to the serving

place and serve topped with the sliced chilli.
Serves 4.
Note: If snow peas are not in season, Chinese broccoli or spinach may be substituted.

Steamed Beef Balls

1 cup raw rice
500 g topside steak,
  minced (see Note)
3 shallots, finely chopped
1 teaspoon finely chopped
  fresh green ginger
2 water chestnuts, finely
  chopped
1 egg, lightly beaten
1 tablespoon soy sauce
2 teaspoons sherry
green vegetable leaves

Place the rice in a bowl, cover with water and soak for about 1 to 1½ hours. Drain well and spread out on a tray to dry.

Combine meat, shallots, ginger, water chestnuts, egg, soy sauce and sherry; mix until well blended. Form the mixture into balls about 4 cm in diameter.

Roll each ball in rice until completely covered. Place balls on green vegetables in steamer basket; they should not touch each other.

Place in a steamer and steam for 30 minutes over gently boiling water. Serve with soy and chilli sauce for dipping
Serves 4.
Note: For best results, buy topside steak and mince it yourself. There are two methods of mincing. *Method one:* Trim the meat and cut into largish pieces. Use one or

two cleavers (one in each hand) and keep chopping until the meat is minced. Place a damp kitchen cloth under the board to deaden the noise. *Method two:* Trim the meat and mince in a processor or use a mincer.

The other ingredients should be very finely chopped.

Chop meat and vegetables finely.

Roll balls in rice until covered.

Place in steamer on green vegetables.

Stir Fried Beef in Black Bean Sauce

500 g rump steak
2 tablespoons fermented
  black beans
2 red peppers
1 onion
4 tablespoons oil
1 clove garlic, finely
  chopped
2 thin slices fresh ginger,
  finely chopped
1 tablespoon sherry
1 teaspoon cornflour
½ cup chicken stock

Crush beans with a pestle and mortar.

Cut peppers into diamond shaped pieces.

Stir fry sliced beef until brown.

Slice beef across the grain into thin strips. Soak black beans in water for about 10 minutes. Drain and crush. Cut peppers into 5 cm strips then cut the strips into 2 cm diamonds. Peel, halve and cut the onion into wedges. Diagonally slice the wedges and separate out into 'diamonds'.

Heat 2 tablespoons of oil in a wok, add garlic and ginger. Stir fry for 1 minute. Add beef, in two batches, and stir fry until the meat changes colour. Remove and keep warm.

Add remaining oil to wok and heat. Add pepper and onion, stir fry for 2 minutes. Add black beans to the wok and stir for 30 seconds.

Blend sherry and cornflour. Pour chicken stock into wok and heat quickly until boiling. Return beef and reheat. Add cornflour mixture and stir fry until thickened. Serves 4.
Note: To mash the beans, use either a mortar and pestle or the handle of a cleaver.

Stir Fried Beef in Black Bean Sauce

PORK

THE meats used in Chinese cookery are pork, beef and lamb. Veal is almost never used, and lamb is rarely served except in the north.

In the course of time the Chinese have developed numerous ways of preparing pork. It can be steamed, braised, red simmered, clear simmered, stir fried, barbequed, roasted and deep fried, and it combines well with a vast number of other ingredients. Leg, shoulder and loin are good choices for almost any of these ways of preparing pork. Other parts of the pig including feet, kidneys, pork belly, etc. are also used extensively in Chinese cooking.

Pork is done when all its pink colour has gone and beef is done when there is no longer any trace of red and the meat is slightly browned. These colour changes are important to watch for, especially in stir fried dishes.

Crisp Roast Belly of Pork

1 kg belly of pork
1 teaspoon salt
1 tablespoon brown sugar
3 tablespoons soy sauce
1 tablespoon hoisin sauce
½ teaspoon grated fresh
   green ginger
2 small firm ripe tomatoes
   (optional)
watercress (optional)

Rub salt into pork skin.

Thoroughly coat meat with sauce.

Grill until skin is crisp.

Prick skin side of pork belly and rub salt into the skin. Mix sugar, soy sauce, hoisin sauce and ginger and rub into the meat side.

Place meat, rind side up, on a rack under a preheated griller and grill for 15 to 20 minutes or until rind is crisp and brown. Place meat, rind side up, on a rack over a baking dish containing about 2 cm water. Roast in a preheated moderate oven (180°C/350°F) for about 1 hour or until cooked when tested. Let cool to room temperature. Garnish with watercress and tomato roses. Note: rind may be removed and served separately. To prepare tomato roses, use a small sharp knife and carefully peel the tomatoes in a circular direction. Coil the strip of tomato to resemble a rose. Secure with a small pin if necessary.
Serves 6.

Crisp Roast Belly of Pork and Bean Curd

1 recipe Roast Belly of
   Pork (see previous
   recipe)
2 cakes bean curd
3 tablespoons soy sauce
½ cup chicken stock
1 tablespoon hoisin sauce
2 tablespoons oil

1 tablespoon cornflour
blended with
2 tablespoons water
few sprigs fresh
   coriander

Prepare roast belly of pork as directed in previous recipe. Cut the pork into cubes.

Cut bean curd cakes into 4 cm slices.

Combine soy sauce, stock and hoisin sauce.

Heat the oil in a wok, add bean curd and stir fry for 1 minute. Add soy sauce mixture, bring to the boil and stir in blended cornflour to thicken. Add the pork and heat through. Serve garnished with coriander.
Serves 6.

Spiced Roast Pork

1.5 kg belly of pork
1½ tablespoons salt
1 teaspoon five spice
   powder
1½ tablespoons cornflour
blended with
1 egg white, lightly beaten

Dipping sauce:
2 tablespoons soy sauce
2 tablespoons vinegar or 2
   tablespoons soy sauce
2 tablespoons sherry

Rub pork with salt and spice. Set aside for a few hours.

Rub the pork all over with cornflour mixture.

Roast pork in preheated hot oven (200°C/400°F) for 1¼ hours until thoroughly cooked. Remove from oven and carve into strips.

Mix together sauce ingredients and serve with pork.
Serves 6.

Sweet and Sour Pork I

2 tablespoons flour
1 egg
1 teaspoon oil
¼ cup water
500 g lean pork, cubed
oil for deep frying
1 green pepper, cubed
3 rings canned pineapple
¾ cup stock
2 tablespoons honey
2 teaspoons soy sauce
¼ cup vinegar
1 tablespoon cornflour
blended with
¼ cup water

Add pork to batter and stir until coated.

Deep fry pork and allow to drain.

Add sauce to vegetables and bring to boil.

Combine first 4 ingredients to make a smooth batter. Stand 10 minutes. Add pork and stir to coat well.

Heat oil for deep frying. Deep fry pork in batches, for 5 minutes; drain well. Reheat the oil and refry the pork until crisp and golden brown. Drain on absorbent paper.

Drain oil leaving about 1 tablespoon in wok.

Heat oil and stir fry green pepper and pineapple for 3 minutes. Add stock, honey, soy sauce and vinegar. Bring to the boil. Add blended cornflour, return to boil and simmer until thickened. Add pork; heat thoroughly. Serve with Chinese Rice.
Serves 4.

Sweet and Sour Pork II

500 g pork shoulder, cubed
2 tablespoons sherry
1 tablespoon soy sauce
¼ teaspoon grated fresh green ginger
6 tablespoons cornflour
oil for deep frying
¼ cucumber
4 celery sticks, sliced
1 red pepper, deseeded and diced
8 shallots, cut into 3 cm pieces

3 tablespoons oil
1 × 440 g can pineapple chunks with juice
¼ cup vinegar
½ cup stock
1 tablespoon brown sugar

Mix the pork with the sherry, soy sauce and ginger. Marinate for 30 minutes.

Heat the oil for deep frying. Remove the pork from the marinade and reserve.

Coat the pork in 4 tablespoons of the cornflour and double fry in the hot oil. Drain well and keep warm.

Halve cucumber lengthwise. Remove seeds and slice thinly. Stir fry all the vegetables in the heated oil for 2 minutes. Drain the pineapple reserving the juice and add the chunks to the wok. Stir fry for 2 minutes.

Mix the remaining cornflour with the vinegar, and stir in to the wok with pineapple juice, stock and sugar. Simmer for 2 minutes, stirring.

Serve the pork on a bed of fried noodles with the sauce poured over.
Serves 4.

Char Sui (Barbecued Pork)

4 tablespoons soy sauce
3 tablespoons dry sherry
6 tablespoons hoisin sauce
2 cloves garlic, crushed
2 teaspoons five spice powder
1 thick slice fresh green ginger, shredded
2 tablespoons brown sugar

2 teaspoons sesame paste
½ cup oil
¼ teaspoon red food colouring
1 kg pork fillet
2 tablespoons honey
2 teaspoons water

Combine soy, sherry and hoisin in a bowl. Stir in garlic, five spice powder, ginger and brown sugar. Blend in sesame paste, oil and food colouring. Pour over pork fillet and marinate overnight, turning occasionally.

Place drained pork on rack in baking dish, containing 1 cm water. Bake in very hot oven (250°C/450°F) for 15 minutes basting frequently. Reduce heat to moderate (180°C/350°F) and bake for a further 15 minutes. Brush with honey and water mixture and cook for a further 5 minutes. Slice thinly. Use as directed in recipes calling for Char Sui.

Tung Po Pork (Steamed Pork)

1 kg pork loin, with rind
4 cups water
5 shallots, cut into 2 cm pieces
⅓ cup soy sauce
2 tablespoons sherry
1 thin slice fresh green ginger, finely chopped
1 tablespoon sugar
½ bunch Chinese cabbage, shredded
1 tablespoon cornflour
blended with
3 tablespoons water

Cut pork into 8 cm squares. Place in wok with the water and bring to boil.

Remove scum from the water. Cover and simmer 30 minutes. Add shallots, soy sauce, sherry and ginger. Cover and simmer for a further 1½ hours.

Remove pork from stock and place, skin side down, in a shallow heatproof dish. Sprinkle with sugar, place in a steamer and steam over gently boiling water 45 minutes.

Meanwhile add cabbage to stock and simmer 10 minutes. With a slotted spoon, transfer cabbage to a serving plate. Top with the pork, skin side up. Serve with a Dipping Sauce.
Serves 4.

Red Simmered Pork

1 fresh squid, cleaned (optional)
1.5 kg shoulder pork, cut into cubes
3 cups water
1 clove garlic, crushed
3 slices fresh green ginger, finely chopped
½ cup soy sauce

1 tablespoon sherry
3 teaspoons brown sugar

Cut the body of the squid in half lengthwise. Score the inside with a sharp knife in a small diamond pattern Cut into 3 cm cubes.

Place pork in a wok, add water and bring to boil over high heat; skim. Add garlic, ginger, soy sauce, and sherry.

Bring to boil, reduce heat, cover and simmer 30 minutes.

Add the squid, cover and simmer 40 minutes more. Add sugar. Cover and simmer for another 30 minutes.
Serves 6.

Braised Pork

1 kg piece boneless pork
  shoulder
2 tablespoons oil
2 slices fresh green
  ginger, finely chopped
1 clove garlic, crushed
6 shallots, cut diagonally
  into 2 cm pieces
½ cup soy sauce
3 tablespoons sherry
3 cups boiling water
2 tablespoons brown
  sugar

Heat oil in a heavy casserole. Brown pork on all sides. Add ginger, garlic and shallots and cook 1 minute.

Add soy sauce, 2 tablespoons sherry and water and bring to a simmer. Reduce heat, cover the pan and simmer 45 minutes, turning the meat every 10 minutes.

Add the remaining sherry and brown sugar and

cook 45 minutes to 1 hour, turning the meat every 20 minutes.

Slice and serve moistened with a little of the cooking liquid.
Serves 4.

Pork Balls with Ginger

8 dried Chinese
  mushrooms
750 g minced lean pork
2.5 cm piece root ginger,
  finely chopped
4 canned water chestnuts,
  finely chopped
1 egg
1 tablespoon soy sauce
4 tablespoons cornflour
⅓ cup oil
extra two tablespoons oil
1 bamboo shoot, diced
1 red pepper, cubed
1 green pepper, cubed

For the sauce:
½ cup vinegar
½ cup sherry
2 tablespoons sugar
2 tablespoons tomato
  sauce
¼–½ teaspoon chilli
  sauce
1 tablespoon soy sauce
3 teaspoons cornflour
blended with
2 tablespoons water

Soak dried mushrooms in hot water for 20 minutes. Drain. Discard stems and slice caps finely.

Combine minced pork with ginger, water chestnuts, egg, soy sauce and 2 tablespoons of the cornflour. Shape into small balls and roll in remaining cornflour.

Heat ⅓ cup oil in wok. Fry the pork balls, in batches, until crisp and brown. Test one to see if it is cooked. Remove and drain on kitchen paper.

Combine all sauce ingredients except cornflour.

Heat the 2 tablespoons oil in wok and stir fry all the vegetables for 3 minutes. Pour over sauce and cook for a further 3 minutes. Thicken with blended cornflour. Pour vegetables and sauce over pork balls.
Serves 4.

Stir Fried Pork, Nuts and Vegetables

500 g lean pork (leg or
  shoulder)
1 tablespoon soy sauce
2 teaspoons cornflour
3 carrots, diagonally sliced
3 tablespoons oil
1 clove garlic, bruised
¼ teaspoon grated fresh
  green ginger
4 stalks celery, sliced
  diagonally
1 small onion, diced
1 red pepper, cut into
  strips
½ cup roasted almonds or
  cashew nuts
1 cup chicken stock
2 tablespoons soy sauce
2 tablespoons sherry
1 teaspoon sesame oil
1 tablespoon cornflour
blended with
3 tablespoons water

Cut meat into thin slices.

Stir fry meat until lightly browned.

Add chopped vegetables and stir fry.

Cut pork into thin slices across the grain.

Mix soy sauce and cornflour. Add pork and toss to coat.

Parboil the carrots for 4 minutes. Rinse under cold running water until completely cooled; drain.

Heat half the oil in a wok. Add pork and stir fry until it has lost any trace of pink. Remove from wok. Add remaining oil and heat. Add garlic and ginger and stir fry until lightly browned. Discard garlic.

Add vegetables and nuts

and stir fry for about 1 minute. Add stock, soy sauce, sherry and sesame oil and bring quickly to the boil.

Reduce heat and simmer for about 2 minutes. Return pork and heat through. Stir in blended cornflour to thicken.
Serves 4.

Stir Fried Pork, Nuts and Vegetab

Barbecued Pork Spareribs

Barbecued Pork Spareribs

1 kg pork spareribs
red and green chillies

Barbecue sauce:
2 cloves garlic, crushed
3 tablespoons soy sauce
1 tablespoon sherry
3 tablespoons hoisin
  sauce
1 tablespoon chicken
  stock
1 tablespoon oil
shallot curls

Combine sauce ingredients. Pour sauce ingredients over the ribs and marinate 3 hours, turning ribs every hour.

Place ribs on a rack over a baking dish containing 2 cm water and roast in a preheated hot oven (200°C/400°F) until cooked when tested. Garnish with shallot curls and chillies.

Serve on a bed of deep fried spring rain noodles (vermicelli).

Serves 4.
Note: Use belly pork cut into strips if spareribs are not available.

Pork and Prawns with Noodles

6 dried Chinese
  mushrooms
500 g noodles
4 tablespoons oil
500 g lean pork, cut in
  strips
250 g shelled school
  prawns
6 shallots, finely sliced
1 garlic clove, crushed
2 tablespoons soy sauce

Soak mushrooms in hot water for 20 minutes. Drain, discard stem and slice caps finely.

Cook the noodles, as directed in Rice and Noodles section. Drain and set aside. Reheat just before serving.

Heat oil in wok, stir fry pork strips about 2 to 3 minutes. Add prawns and stir fry further 2 minutes. Add shallots, garlic, mushrooms

and stir fry constantly for 2 minutes. Stir in soy sauce. Serve over noodles.
Serves 6.

Smoked Chicke

CHICKEN AND DUCK

DUCK and chicken are the favourite birds in China. As with beef and pork the Chinese have created many interesting ways of preparing their poultry. Drying, smoking and curing are methods used with duck as well as roasting, simmering, steaming and, of course, stir frying. Many of the same methods are used for chicken.

When a recipe calls for a whole chicken, purchase a size 15 chicken (or 1.5 kg). Use fresh chickens whenever possible. Remove any fat from the body cavity, wash well under cold water and dry with paper towel. It is most important, when using a whole chicken in any type of recipe, to clean the area between the back bones; use the handle of a teaspoon to scrape out any matter and wipe with a damp cloth.

Whole chickens from Chinese speciality shops often come complete with head and feet. The reason for this is that the beak and feet give an indication as to the age of a chicken — they should be pliable. Simply cut the neck and feet off and use in the stock pot.

If using a frozen chicken, make sure it is completely defrosted before cooking. **Do not** defrost the chicken in the refrigerator — this will take up to 24 hours. Follow the same cleaning procedures as for fresh chicken.

The same cleaning rules apply to both fresh and frozen duck. When purchasing a fresh duck, make sure the oil sacs in the tail have been removed before cooking. Ducks are sometimes trussed and immersed in boiling water to remove the excess oil that duck, as a water bird, has under its skin. Always pierce the skin of a whole duck several times before cooking.

Step-by-step instructions for chopping a chicken Chinese style are in the techniques section in the front of the book. The Chinese always chop the backbone and serve this with the rest of the meat. When chopping a cooked bird always wear an apron!

Smoked Chicken

1 × size 15 chicken
2 tablespoons brown
  peppercorns
1 tablespoon salt
8 cups water
4 shallots
3 slices green ginger
2 whole star anise
1 cinnamon stick
1 cup soy sauce
½ cup sugar
½ cup flour
½ cup tea leaves
1 tablespoon sesame oil

Clean and wipe chicken. Fry the peppercorn and salt for 1 minute. Rub into the chicken and allow to stand for 2 hours.

Bring water to the boil in a large pan. Add shallots, ginger, star anise, cinnamon and soy sauce and simmer for 10 minutes. Add the chicken to the simmering liquid and cook for 10 minutes over a low heat, turning once. Remove chicken and allow to cool.

Put sugar, flour and tea leaves in base of wok, and cover with a rack. Sit chicken on its side on rack. Cover tightly and smoke for 20 to 30 minutes over a low heat, turning chicken halfway through. Remove chicken from pan and brush with sesame oil. Cool.

Chop Chinese style (see Techniques) and arrange on platter.
Serves 6.

Stir Fried Chicken

4 dried Chinese
  mushrooms
1 onion
1 red pepper
2.5 cm piece fresh green
  ginger, peeled and sliced
2 whole chicken breasts
6 tablespoons oil
1 × 220 g can water
  chestnuts, drained and
  quartered
250 g bean sprouts
1 teaspoon cornflour
¾ cup chicken stock
1 tablespoon soy sauce
1 tablespoon oyster sauce
2 teaspoons dry sherry

Cover mushrooms with hot water and soak for 20 minutes. Remove the stalk and discard then halve the caps. Quarter the onion and separate into layers. Cut the red pepper into strips and thinly slice the ginger.

Skin and bone chicken breasts and cut into pieces. Heat 3 tablespoons of the oil in a wok and stir fry the chicken until cooked through. Drain on absorbent paper.

Heat the remaining oil in a pan, add ginger and water chestnuts and stir fry for 3 minutes. Add the onion, red pepper and bean sprouts and stir fry for 2 minutes.

Add the chicken stock, soy and oyster sauces and sherry. Simmer for a few minutes.

Dissolve the cornflour in a little water and add to the wok with the chicken. Heat until the sauce is thick and the chicken hot.

Serve with boiled rice.
Serves 4.

Lemon Chicken

1 × size 15 chicken
2 tablespoons soy sauce
3 teaspoons sugar
2 tablespoons sherry
4 lemons
4 tablespoons oil
1 slice green ginger, fried
2 cloves garlic, crushed
1½ cups stock
2 teaspoons cornflour
  blended with 2
  tablespoons water
coriander

Chop chicken Chinese style (see Techniques). Combine the soy sauce, sugar, sherry and ½ cup (freshly squeezed) lemon juice. Brush over chicken and allow to stand for 1 hour.

Heat wok, add oil, heat and add ginger and garlic. Stir fry chicken, in batches, until brown. Pour in stock and remaining marinade. Simmer, covered, for 10 to 15 minutes or until chicken is tender. Remove chicken onto serving plate.

Stir blended cornflour into stock and bring to boil. Spoon sauce over chicken and garnish with coriander and thinly sliced lemon.
Serves 6.

White Cooked Chicken

1 × size 15 chicken
water to cover
½ bunch shallots, cut into
  pieces
3 slices fresh green ginger
1 recipe Sherry-Soy Dip
  Sauce

Truss the chicken and place it whole into a large wok with enough boiling water to cover. Add shallots and ginger slices. Bring to boil, reduce the heat, cover and cook the chicken for 12 minutes. Turn the chicken, cover and simmer another 10 minutes.

Remove the wok from the heat and allow the chicken to cool in the liquid. Cut the chicken legs and wings into 5 cm sections, cutting through the bone with a heavy cleaver. Arrange slices of breast meat in the centre of a serving plate. Place the sections of wing, leg and thigh around the breast. Serve cold with Sherry-Soy Dip Sauce.
Serves 6.
Note: The thrifty Chinese would flavour the stock and serve it as a soup. Alternatively, strain and keep as stock.

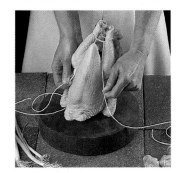
Truss chicken.

Add ginger and shallots and bring to boil.

Chop chicken into 5 cm pieces.

White Cooked Chicken

Sweet and Sour Sesame Chicken

1 × size 15 chicken, jointed
3 tablespoons plum sauce
1 tablespoon vinegar
2 cups chicken stock
⅓ cup dry sherry
1 tablespoon finely chopped fresh green ginger
1 onion, quartered
160 g canned straw mushrooms
2 sticks celery, sliced
1 × 220 g can water chestnuts
1 × 220 g can bamboo shoots, drained and sliced
2 tablespoons cornflour
1 tablespoon sesame seeds

Set oven temperature to moderate (180°C/350°F).

Arrange chicken in ovenproof dish. Combine the plum sauce, vinegar, stock, sherry and ginger and pour over chicken. Cover and bake 40 minutes.

Add the vegetables, return to oven and cook a further 15 minutes. Remove chicken and vegetables to heated serving dish.

Thicken remaining liquid with cornflour blended with a little water. Bring to boil and simmer 2 minutes. Pour over chicken. Sprinkle with sesame seeds and serve hot with Chinese Rice.
Serves 6.

Chicken with Mushrooms

2 whole chicken breasts, skinned, boned and cut into cubes
1 tablespoon cornflour
2 tablespoons oil
¼ teaspoon grated fresh green ginger
125 g canned straw mushrooms
1 green pepper, seeded and cut into strips

Toss the chicken pieces in the cornflour. Heat the oil in a wok until very hot. Add ginger and stir fry 30 seconds. Add chicken and stir fry until white. Remove chicken from the wok. Add mushrooms and green pepper and stir fry 1½ minutes.

Return chicken to the wok and stir until heated through.
Serves 4.
Note: If fresh oyster mushrooms are available, these can be added to the dish. Fresh mushrooms are not a suitable substitute as the flavour of the dish will completely change.

Braised Chicken in Soy Sauce

1 × size 15 chicken
¾ cup soy sauce
3 tablespoons sherry
1½ cups chicken stock
3 tablespoons oil
½ bunch shallots, cut into 2 cm pieces
1 clove garlic, crushed
½ teaspoon grated fresh green ginger

Cut chicken through the bone with a cleaver into 5 cm pieces. Combine soy sauce, sherry and chicken stock. Bring to boil, cover and remove from heat. Heat oil in a wok, add chicken and stir fry until lightlly browned on all sides. Add shallots, garlic and ginger and stir fry for 1 minute. Add hot soy sauce mixture and return to boiling point. Reduce the heat. Cover and simmer for 40 minutes. Place chicken in a serving dish. Strain sauce and add a little of the sauce to the chicken.
Note: Chicken may be trussed and cooked whole. Chop Chinese style to serve (see Techniques section.)
Serves 4.

Deep Fried Chicken Balls

2 whole chicken breasts, skinned, boned and minced
6 shallots, finely chopped
2 tablespoons soy sauce
2 tablespoons sherry
2 tablespoons cornflour
2 egg yolks
1 egg white
oil for deep frying

Combine all the ingredients, except the egg white and oil, and mix until blended. Beat the egg white until stiff and fold into the chicken mixture. Chill 1 hour.

Heat oil for deep frying. Form chicken mixture into small ovals and deep fry, in batches, for 3 minutes. Remove with a skimmer and drain. Reheat the oil and deep fry the chicken, in batches, until golden brown. Drain well on paper towel. Serve with Sweet Sour Sauce.
Serves 4.

Deep Fried Chicken

1 × size 15 chicken
boiling water
4 tablespoons soy sauce
2 tablespoons sherry
2 teaspoons grated fresh
green ginger
oil for deep frying

Place the chicken into boiling water, spoon water over the breast and immediately lift it out. Wipe completely dry with paper towel. Mix soy, sherry and ginger and brush the chicken with this mixture inside and out.

Heat the oil for deep frying. Using a skimmer and a pair of tongs, lower chicken into hot oil and deep fry for about 10 minutes, turning occasionally. Lift out chicken and cool for 10 minutes. Reheat oil, return chicken and deep fry for another 8 to 10 minutes. Lift out chicken and cool for 10 minutes. Reheat oil, return chicken and deep fry for another 8 to 10 minutes or until golden brown and done.

Lift out and drain well on paper towel. Chop Chinese style (see Techniques section). Arrange on a platter. Serve with a dip sauce made by combining 3 tablespoons sherry, 1 tablespoon soy sauce, 1 teaspoon chili sauce and ¼ teaspoon sugar, mixed until well blended.
Serves 4.
Serve with noodles.
Note: If liked, the marinade can be diluted with ½ cup stock, and brought to the boil; thicken and serve as a sauce with the chicken.

Blanch chicken in boiling water.

Coat with seasoning mixture.

Deep fry chicken, turning occasionally.

Deep Fried Chicken

Steamed Chicken and Sausages

1 × size 15 chicken
2 tablespoons sherry
1 teaspoon soy sauce
1 tablespoon cornflour
1 pair larp cheong
  (Chinese sausages), cut
  into thick diagonal slices

With a cleaver, chop chicken into 5 cm pieces. Combine sherry, soy sauce and cornflour and toss chicken pieces in this mixture. Transfer chicken to a shallow dish and place sausage slices in between and on top of the chicken pieces. Place dish in a steamer and steam 45 minutes to 1 hour or until chicken is tender.
Serves 4.

Steamed Chicken and Ham

2 large chicken breasts,
  boned, but not skinned
2 × 1 cm thick slices lean,
  smoked ham
6 dried Chinese
  mushrooms
3 teaspoons soy sauce
1 tablespoon oil
1 tablespoon sherry
green vegetable leaves

Cut chicken breasts crosswise into 1 cm thick slices. (Make sure the skin remains attached to the meat.)
  Cut the ham into as many slices as there are pieces of chicken and in approximately the same shape.
  Soak the mushrooms in hot water for 20 minutes and squeeze dry. Cut off the stalks and cut the caps in half.
  Sprinkle the chicken slices with combined soy and oil. Sprinkle the ham slices with sherry. Line a steamer with green vegetable leaves and place rows of alternating chicken slices (skin side up) and ham slices on top. Surround with mushroom halves or arrange mushrooms between chicken and ham. Steam over gently boiling water for 25 minutes or until tender. Serve hot.
Serves 4.

Drunken Chicken

6 cups water
½ bunch shallots, cut in
  1 cm lengths
6 slices fresh green
  ginger, shredded
1 × size 15 chicken,
  trussed
2 tablespoons soy sauce
1 cup sherry

Bring the water to the boil in a wok and add shallots, ginger and chicken. Reduce heat, cover and simmer 25 minutes. Remove from the heat and leave 20 more minutes. Drain chicken and place in a bowl with soy and sherry. Cover with foil and refrigerate at least 1 day.
  To serve, drain chicken and chop Chinese style (see Techniques section.)
Serves 4.
Note: This recipe should traditionally be cooked with Chinese wine but dry sherry is a good substitute. Drunken chicken and soy chicken are the two chickens usually seen hanging in Chinese store windows.
Note: This recipe should traditionally be cooked with Chinese wine but dry sherry is a good substitute. Drunken Chicken and Soy Chicken are the two chickens usually seen hanging in Chinese store windows.

Yu Lang Chi (Chicken with Broccoli)

1.5 litres chicken stock
2.5 cm piece fresh green
  ginger, peeled and sliced
2 shallots, cut into 5 cm
  pieces
1 × size 15 chicken,
  trussed
4 slices ham, cut into thin
  strips
1 kg broccoli, trimmed
1 teaspoon cornflour
blended with
1 tablespoon water
2 teaspoons soy sauce

In a wok combine chicken stock, ginger and shallots. Bring liquid to the boil. Add the chicken and bring to the boil again. Reduce heat, cover and simmer for 30 minutes.
  Turn off heat and allow chicken to cook, tightly covered, for 2 hours.
  Take chicken from wok, drain well and place on a board. Remove skin and carve chicken meat into strips and arrange with ham on a dish. Keep warm.
  Discard all but 2 cups of the liquid. Bring stock to the boil, add broccoli and bring to the boil again. Turn off heat and allow to stand in stock for 5 minutes. Drain broccoli, reserving ½ cup stock. Arrange around chicken. Keep warm.
  To make sauce, mix cornflour and soy sauce and add to reserved stock. Bring to the boil, stirring continuously. Pour sauce over chicken and serve immediately.
Serves 6.
Note: All the broccoli should be used, not just the heads. Peel the stalks, using a small sharp knife, and trim. Diagonally slice the stalks and cook with the broccoli heads.

risp

Peking Duck

1 × 2 kg duck
boiling water
½ to ¾ cup water
4 tablespoons honey
1 recipe Peking Doilies
shallot curls
½ cucumber
½ to ¾ cup hoisin sauce
  or plum sauce

Blanch duck in boiling water.

Baste thoroughly with honey sauce.

Remove skin and carve meat into thick slices.

Choose a fresh duck with neck and skin intact. Wash duck, immerse in boiling water, lift out and dry thoroughly inside and out. Hang the bird overnight in a cool airy place to allow the skin to dry thoroughly.

Dissolve honey in water and brush skin until completely saturated with honey. Hang the duck to dry completely for about 6 hours or until the skin is dry and slightly hardened by the honey.

Meanwhile, prepare Peking doilies and shallot curls. Peel cucumber and cut in half lengthwise. Scoop out the seedy centre part and cut into strips.

To separate the skin from the flesh of duck, insert a straw and blow through it. Place duck on a rack over a drip pan. Roast in a 180°C (350°F) oven without basting for about 1 to 1¼ hours or until skin is browned and crisp.

With a very sharp knife, slice off skin and cut into squares. Carve meat in thick slices and serve separately during the same meal. Take a doily and top with one or two pieces of skin, shallot curls, hoisin or plum sauce and cucumber strips. Roll doily to eat.
Note: Sometimes only the skin is eaten and the meat used as an ingredient for other dishes. Serves 6.

Red Simmered Chicken

1 × size 15 chicken
2 thin slices fresh green
  ginger, finely chopped
1 clove garlic, crushed
2 whole star anise
2 tablespoons sherry
½ cup soy sauce
½ cup chicken stock
2 teaspoons sesame oil
shallot curls

Wash chicken well. Dry chicken thoroughly, inside and out, with paper towels and truss. In a wok, combine all the remaining ingredients. Bring to a boil and add the chicken. Reduce the heat, cover and simmer 1 to 1½ hours or until cooked, turning the chicken every 15 minutes.

Drain chicken and cut into 5 cm pieces.

Decorate with shallot curls and serve.
Serves 4.

Red Simmered Duck

2 pieces dried tangerine
  peel
1 × 2 kg duck
½ teaspoon green ginger
½ bunch shallots, roughly
  chopped
6 tablespoons soy sauce
4 tablespoons sherry
1 whole star anise
1 teaspoon sugar

Soak the tangerine peel in warm water for 25 minutes and drain.

Wipe the duck well and pierce the thigh section several times with a skewer. Place the duck on its back in a large wok. Add water to cover and bring to boil. Cook for 3 to 4 minutes. Skim stock carefully.

Add tangerine peel,

ginger, shallots, soy sauce, sherry, star anise and sugar. Return to boil, reduce heat, cover and simmer about 50 to 60 minutes. Turn the duck over and simmer for another 30 to 40 minutes or until completely tender.

Lift the duck from the wok with a skimmer. Drain and cut the duck through the bone into 5 cm pieces with a

cleaver. Strain the cooking liquid and serve a little of the liquid with the duck to moisten it. The remaining liquid can be used for preparation of other red cooked dishes.
Serves 6.
Note: A strip of orange rind may be substituted for the dried tangerine peel.

eking Doilies with Peking Duck

Ho Tao Chi Tin

Ho Tao Chi Tin (Chicken with Walnuts)

500 g chicken breasts
1 tablespoon cornflour
1 egg white, lightly beaten
1 cup oil
250 g walnut halves
1 teaspoon sugar
1 tablespoon soy sauce
2 tablespoons dry sherry

Skin and bone chicken breasts, and cut meat into strips. Mix cornflour and egg white. Add chicken and coat evenly on all sides.

Heat the oil in a wok. Deep fry the chicken, in batches, for 2 minutes; drain well. Reheat the oil and deep fry the chicken until golden. Drain and keep warm on a serving dish. Pour off all but 1 tablespoon oil from wok. Add walnuts, reduce heat and stir fry for 1 minute.

Remove and sprinkle over the chicken.

Add sugar, soy sauce and sherry and simmer for 2 minutes. Remove from heat and pour over the chicken or serve separately.

Garnish with coriander leaves and sliced red chilli. Serves 4.

Note: Walnuts are often bitter when fried. To remove the bitterness they can be peeled. Simmer for 1 minute then drain and remove the skin with a skewer. Dry thoroughly.

Stir Fried Roast Duck and Mixed Meats

Stir Fried Roast Duck and Mixed Meats

500 g red roast duck
125 g Char Sui
½ chicken breast, skinned
  and boned
125 g lean smoked ham
90 g chicken livers,
  cleaned
1 onion
3 tablespoons oil
1 clove garlic, crushed
2 thin slices fresh green
  ginger
½ bunch shallots, cut into
  1 cm diagonal slices
1 cup chicken stock
1 tablespoon soy sauce
2 tablespoons sherry
2 teaspoons cornflour
blended with
3 tablespoons water

Cut duck, pork, chicken and
ham into 5 × 2 × 1 cm thick
pieces.
  Bring 2 cups salted water
to boil and add the chicken
livers. Reduce heat and
simmer 5 to 6 minutes until
firm then drain and cut into
6 mm slices. Cut onion in
1 cm wide wedges.
  Heat the oil in a wok.
Add garlic and ginger and stir
fry until lightly browned.
Discard garlic and ginger. Add
shallots and onion and stir fry
for 30 seconds. Add ham,
chicken livers and chicken
and stir fry for another
minute. Add roast duck and
roast pork and stir fry to heat
through. Pour in stock, soy,
and sherry and bring to a boil.
Stir in blended cornflour to
thicken. Transfer to a serving
dish and garnish with
coriander, if liked.

Note: Shredded bamboo and
bean sprouts may be added.
They should be stir fried with
the onion, then removed from
the wok and added with the
stock to heat through. Sliced
fresh green or red ginger may
also be added.
Serves 6.

Duck with Pineapple

1 × 2.5 kg duck
1 clove garlic, peeled
3 tablespoons oil
1 × 440 g can pineapple
  slices
½ cup pineapple juice
  from can
1 cup chicken or duck
  stock
1 teaspoon cornflour
blended with
2 tablespoons water

For sauce:
4 tablespoons soy sauce
1 tablespoon sugar
2 teaspoons vinegar
1 tablespoon sherry
2 thin slices ginger, finely
  chopped

Wash duck and wipe well. Remove any excess fat and pierce the skin of the duck several times with a skewer. Heat oil in a wok and brown duck all over. Pour off any surplus oil. Add the pineapple juice and stock to the wok. Cover and simmer gently for about 1 hour or until the duck is cooked. Remove and keep warm.

Clean wok. Add sauce ingredients and bring to boil; thicken with blended cornflour.

Spoon sauce over duck and garnish with the sliced pineapple. Serve with Fried Rice.
Serves 6–8.

Stir Fried Duck Slices and Bitter Melon

1 tablespoon fermented
  black beans
1 clove garlic
1 × 2 kg duck
1 tablespoon hoisin sauce
1 tablespoon sherry
½ teaspoon chilli sauce
1 tablespoon cornflour
250 g fresh bitter melon
  (or ½ 450 g can bitter
  melon)
4 tablespoons oil
1 cup chicken stock
extra 2 teaspoons
  cornflour
2 tablespoons water

Soak black beans in water for 10 minutes. Drain and mash the beans with the garlic. Cut the duck meat from the breast and legs and reserve carcass for making stock. Cut meat across the grain into 1 cm thick slices.

Mix hoisin sauce, sherry, chilli sauce and cornflour. Add duck slices and mix well. Marinate for 20 minutes.

When using fresh bitter melon, wash and drain. Remove stalks, halve bitter melon lengthwise and remove seedy centre. Cut into thin slices. Bring plenty of salted water to boil, add bitter melon and parboil 4 minutes.

Rinse under cold running water until completely cooled. Drain. When using canned bitter melon, drain liquid, rinse under cold running water, drain and slice.

Heat half the oil in a wok. Add black bean mixture and stir fry for 30 seconds. Add duck slices and stir fry until lightly coloured. Remove and keep warm. Add remaining oil, heat and stir fry the bitter melon for 1 to 1½ minutes. Add stock and bring to a boil. Return duck slices to the wok, reduce heat, cover and simmer until heated through. Blend cornflour with water and add to wok; cook until sauce is thickened.
Serves 4–6.

Chicken with Chillies

2 tablespoons soy sauce
1 egg white, lightly beaten
2 tablespoons cornflour
2 whole chicken breasts,
  skinned & boned
1 tablespoon red wine
  vinegar
1 teaspoon soy sauce
2 teaspoons sesame seed
  paste
⅓ cup oil
1 clove garlic, bruised
2 thin slices fresh green
  ginger, shredded
2 chilli peppers, seeded
  and sliced
1 green pepper, seeded
  and cubed

Combine the soy sauce, sherry, egg white and cornflour in a bowl.

Cut the chicken into strips, add to the bowl and stir to coat evenly with the egg white mixture.

Combine the vinegar, soy & sesame seed paste. Heat the oil in a wok, add the garlic and ginger and fry until golden; remove and discard.

Add the chillies and chicken and stir fry until the chicken is golden. Add the green pepper and stir fry for 30 seconds. Add the vinegar mixture and stir fry until the sauce thickens.

Serve with Chinese Rice.
Serves 4.

SEAFOOD

THE aim in cooking fish is to produce as natural a flavour as possible from the freshest fish available. Both fresh water and salt water fish are used and in comparison with the Western style of cooking, more emphasis is placed on the fresh water varieties. One aspect of fish cooking which seems strange to Western people is that cleaning and scaling are often the only preparations done ahead and, quite contrary to the general practice in the West, the fish is usually left whole, with complete head, tail and fins. Aesthetic arguments aside, it is undoubtedly true that leaving the fish intact improves the flavour. Steaming as well as clear simmering are favourite ways of cooking fish because the subtle natural flavour is retained and the flesh is both tender and moist. However, deep frying, braising and even stir frying are methods which are also used. Fish which is to be deep fried is either dredged in flour or cornflour or is coated with a batter to seal in all of the juices. To eliminate the 'fishy' taste, a number of seasonings can be used with the fish. Ginger, garlic, shallots, black beans, soy sauce and wine are the most popular. The fish is often scored to permit the flavours to be absorbed better and to expose a greater cooking surface.

Besides fish, the Chinese also eat a great deal of other seafood including prawns, crab, lobster, scallops, clams and oysters. They are also fond of sea cucumber, squid and sea urchins.

Prolonged cooking tends to make seafood both tough and unpalatable, so the techniques used for cooking it are generally restricted to stir frying, deep frying, and steaming. Though fresh seafood is generally preferable, frozen seafood can be substituted successfully. Canned abalone need only be heated very briefly. Special care which needs to be taken in preparing various types of seafood is given in the recipes.

Prawns Chow Mein

10 dried Chinese mushrooms, soaked in hot water 20 minutes
2 tablespoons oil
2 sticks celery, sliced
125 g bamboo shoots, sliced
250 g bean sprouts, washed
250 g water chestnuts, drained and sliced
½ cup chicken stock
1 tablespoon dry sherry
1 tablespoon soy sauce
500 g school prawns, shelled

Drain mushrooms, squeeze dry and discard stalks. Slice into strips. Heat oil in wok. Add celery, bamboo shoots, mushrooms, bean sprouts, and water chestnuts. Stir fry about 2 minutes until vegetables are tender but crisp.

Pour in stock and wine. Increase to high and bring to the boil. Reduce heat and stir in soy sauce and prawns. Cover and cook for 3 minutes. Remove from heat and serve immediately.
Serves 4.

Prawns Chow Mein

Prawns with Bean Sprouts

250 g firm white fish fillets
½ cup flour
½ cup oil
extra 2 tablespoons oil
1 onion, sliced
5 dried Chinese
  mushrooms, soaked and
  sliced
1 clove garlic, crushed
250 g cooked peeled
  school prawns
500 g bean sprouts
1 teaspoon soy sauce

Skin fish fillets, cut into strips and dip in flour. Heat oil in wok. Fry fish in batches until golden; drain. Heat extra oil in wok. Stir fry onion. Add mushrooms and garlic. Stir fry gently for 4 minutes.

Add bean sprouts. Stir fry gently about 4 minutes. Add soy sauce, prawns and fish. Stir fry 2 minutes. Serve on a bed of Braised Vegetables (see recipe.) Serves 4.

Stir Fried Crab, Ginger and Shallots

2 large live crabs
2 tablespoons oil
1 clove garlic, crushed
3 thin slices fresh ginger
  root, finely chopped
1 bunch shallots, sliced
¾ cup chicken stock
1 tablespoon soy sauce
1 tablespoon sherry
¼ teaspoon sugar
⅛ teaspoon sesame oil
2 teaspoons cornflour
blended with
2 tablespoons water

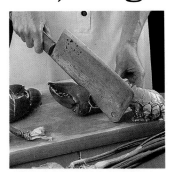
Crack crab claws using blunt edge of cleaver.

Separate crabmeat from the shell.

Add crab pieces and stir fry.

Scrub the crabs in water. Steam or simmer for 20 minutes. Drain and cool.

Twist off claws and legs and crack the legs. With a chopping knife or cleaver, chop claws in half and crack. Separate the body from the shell and discard all soft, spongy parts. Chop body into large pieces.

Heat the oil in a wok. Add garlic and ginger and stir fry for ½ minute. Add crab pieces and stir fry to coat with oil. Pour in stock, soy sauce, sherry, sugar and sesame oil and bring quickly to boil.

Stir in the blended cornflour, bring to the boil. Serves 4.

Stir Fried Crab, Ginger and Shallots

Stir Fried Abalone

12 small dried Chinese
  mushrooms
2 × 145 g cans abalone
6 tablespoons oil
2 small onions, cut into
  strips
½ cup chicken stock
8 tablespoons abalone
  liquid reserved from the
  cans

2 tablespoons sherry
½ teaspoon sesame oil
1 teaspoon cornflour
  dissolved in
2 tablespoons water

Soak the dried Chinese mushrooms in hot water for 20 minutes. Squeeze dry. Cut off the stems and leave the caps whole.

Drain the abalone. Cut into 3 mm thick slices.

Heat the oil in a wok. Add mushroom caps and onion. Stir fry for 1½ minutes. Add chicken stock, abalone liquid, sherry and sesame oil. Bring to boil.

Add abalone. (Do not cook the abalone too long or it will toughen.) Stir in blended cornflour to thicken sauce.
Serves 4.

Stir Fried Lobster and Pork

1 green (1 kg) lobster
3 tablespoons oil
1 clove garlic, crushed
1 thin slice fresh ginger,
  finely chopped
2 tablespoons soy sauce
1 tablespoon sherry
¼ teaspoon sesame oil
175 g lean pork, minced
4 tablespoons chicken
  stock
1 egg, beaten

Chop lobster in half.

Stir fry lobster until flesh is white.

Fry pork mixture until brown.

Place the lobster on its back on a chopping board. Chop with a heavy cleaver down its entire length. Chop tail into 5 cm pieces. Cut legs in half and chop each claw into 3 pieces.

Heat oil in wok. Stir in garlic and ginger. Add lobster, stir fry for 2½ minutes until shell is bright red and the lobster meat is white and opaque. Remove the lobster.

Combine soy sauce, sherry and sesame oil with the pork. Stir fry for 2 minutes or until pork has lost any trace of pink. Return lobster to wok.

Add chicken stock and heat to boiling point. Stir in egg and stir fry 30 seconds.
Serves 4.

Stir Fried Squid and Vegetables

500 g calamari
125 g Chinese celery
  cabbage
2 thin slices fresh green
  ginger
1 onion, cut into wedges
2 dried Chinese
  mushrooms, soaked and
  sliced
½ cup chicken stock
1 tablespoon soy sauce
2 teaspoons cornflour
  blended with
1 tablespoon water
3 tablespoons oil

Rinse calamari under cold water.

Hold in right hand and pull tentacles and intestines out with left hand, discard. Rub with salted fingers to remove skin. Wash under cold water. Cut the calamari in half lengthwise and score inside flesh in diamond pattern. Cut the cabbage into thick slices; finely chop the ginger.

Heat the oil in the wok; stir fry the calamari for 1 minute; remove. Stir fry the onion, ginger, cabbage and mushrooms. Add the chicken stock, soy sauce and blended cornflour; stir until boiling.

Replace the calamari and cook until heated through.
Serves 4.

Stir Fried Prawns and Bean Sprouts

2 tablespoons oil
2 slices fresh green ginger
500 g shelled Royal Red
  prawns
1 onion, cut into wedges
6 shallots, sliced
125 g bean sprouts

1 cup chicken stock
2 teaspoons soy sauce
1 tablespoon sherry
1 tablespoon cornflour
blended with
2 tablespoons water

Heat the oil in a wok, add ginger and stir fry for 30 seconds. Add the prawns and onion and stir fry for 1½ minutes. Add shallots and bean sprouts and stir fry for another 1 minute.

Stir in combined chicken stock, soy sauce, sherry and bring quickly to boil. Stir in blended cornflour to thicken and serve.
Serves 4–6.

Deep Fried Prawns

750 g large prawns

Batter:
3 tablespoons flour
1 tablespoon cornflour
1 egg, lightly beaten
1 teaspoon salt
1 teaspoon sherry
4 tablespoons water

Sauce:
¼ cup soy sauce
¼ cup tomato sauce
1 teaspoon brown sugar
1 teaspoon lemon juice
¼ teaspoon tabasco
  sauce

Oil for deep frying
6 shallot curls, for garnish
½ cup plum sauce
¼ cup salt and pepper mix

Shell and devein prawns leaving the tail intact. Combine the batter ingredients and beat until smooth.

Mix the sauce ingredients until well blended.

Heat the oil for deep frying. Holding the prawns by the tail, dip them into the batter to coat lightly and drop into the hot oil one by one. Fry until golden brown and drain on paper towels.

Serve with shallot garnish, sauces and salt and

pepper mix on the side.
Serves 4–6.

Shell prawns and remove veins.

Coat prawns with batter. Deep fry battered prawns and allow to drain.

Deep Fried Prawns

Honeyed Prawns

2 tablespoons oil
1 clove garlic, crushed
1 slice fresh green ginger,
    shredded
750 g green prawns,
    shelled but leave tail
    intact

¼ cup honey
2 teaspoons soy sauce
sesame seeds

Heat oil in wok. Add garlic and ginger and stir fry for 30 seconds. Add prawns in two batches and stir fry until pink. Remove the first batch before cooking the second batch. Pour over combined honey and soy sauce, toss quickly.
Serve sprinkled with sesame seeds.

Deep Fried Prawns and Sweet and Sour Sauce

500 g large prawns
1 recipe Sweet Sour
    Sauce
3 tablespoons flour
½ tablespoon cornflour
1 egg
½ teaspoon sherry
½ teaspoon finely
    chopped ginger root
3 tablespoons water
Oil for deep frying

Shell and devein prawns. Cut prawns into 3 cm pieces. Prepare the Sweet Sour Sauce and keep warm.
    Mix flour, cornflour, egg, sherry, ginger root and water into a smooth batter.
    Heat the oil for deep frying. Dip prawn pieces in the batter to coat lightly and deep fry, dropping in the hot oil one by one, until golden brown.
    Drain on paper towels. Transfer to a serving dish. Serve with hot Sweet Sour Sauce.
Serves 4–6.

Fish Balls

750 g gemfish fillets
2 thin slices fresh ginger,
    finely grated
½ cup water
1 tablespoon sherry
2 tablespoons finely
    chopped shallot
1 tablespoon soy sauce
2 egg whites
1 teaspoon cornflour

Skin and bone gemfish fillets.
    Beat the fish and ginger until smooth, adding half the water gradually. Add sherry, shallot and soy sauce. Beat well.
    Add egg whites and cornflour and beat vigorously 1 minute. Add more water gradually if the mixture seems very stiff.
    Divide the mixture to form 16 small balls.
    Bring 1 litre of stock or water to boil. Reduce heat, drop in the fish balls and poach in simmering water for 6 minutes. Remove with skimmer and serve hot with chilli or soy sauce.
Serves 4.

Steamed Bream with Black Beans

1 × 1.5 kg whole bream
1½ to 2 tablespoons
    fermented black beans
1 clove garlic, crushed
2 thin slices fresh green
    ginger, finely chopped
6 shallots, finely sliced
3 tablespoons soy sauce
1 tablespoon sherry
½ teaspoon sugar
1 tablespoon oil
6 shallot curls

Clean and scale fish. Score crosswise on both sides.
    Soak the fermented black beans in water for about 20 minutes. Drain and mash together with garlic.
    Place fish in a shallow heatproof dish. Mix all ingredients except shallot curls until blended and spread over fish. Place in a steamer and steam for about 30 minutes or until tender.
    Remove from steamer. Decorate with shallot curls and serve.
Serves 4.

Crab with Straw Mushrooms

3 tablespoons oil
3 slices fresh green ginger
2 shallots, sliced
1 tablespoon dry sherry
1 tablespoon soy sauce
1 × 225 g can crab meat

1 × 225 g can straw
  mushrooms, drained
½ cup chicken stock
1 teaspoon cornflour
blended with
1 tablespoon water

Heat oil in wok and stir fry the ginger and shallots.

Add the sherry, soy sauce and crab meat and stir fry for 1 minute.

Add the mushrooms and stock, bring to the boil and simmer for 1 minute.

Stir in the blended cornflour and bring to the boil.

Serves 4.

Braised Bream and Bean Curd

1 kg whole bream (or
  schnapper)
3 tablespoons flour
½ cup oil
2 thin slices fresh green
  ginger root
6 shallots, chopped
3 tablespoons soy sauce
1 tablespoon sherry
¾ cup chicken stock

¼ teaspoon sesame oil
2 teaspoons oyster sauce
1½ to 2 cakes bean curd,
  cut into 2 cm cubes

Clean and scale the fish. Remove fins and trim tail. Wash fish under cold running water, drain and dry. Score on both sides.

Coat fish evenly with flour. Heat the oil in a large wok. Add the ginger and shallots and stir fry until golden. Fry fish over high heat until brown on both sides. Remove excess oil. Sprinkle with soy sauce and sherry.

Add chicken stock, sesame oil and oyster sauce, bring to a boil quickly. Reduce heat, add bean curd, cover and simmer for 8 to 10 minutes.
Serves 4–6.

Garlic Prawns with Vegetables

¼ cup oil
3 cloves garlic, crushed
500 g green prawns,
  shelled and deveined
250 g broccoli, broken into
  flowerets
2 sticks celery, sliced
  diagonally
½ red capsicum, diced
1 × 440 g can baby corn,
  drained
60 g bamboo shoots, cut
  in shapes
2 shallots, cut in 3 cm
  pieces
2 teaspoons soy sauce
2 tablespoons dry sherry
¼ cup chicken stock

Heat wok, add oil and garlic, cook 2–3 minutes. Add prawns and stir fry until just pink. Remove and set aside.

Stir fry broccoli 2–3 minutes, add celery and capsicum, stir fry 3 minutes. Add corn, bamboo shoots and shallots and heat through. Add liquids and bring to the boil. Return prawns and serve immediately.

If desired thicken with a little cornflour blended in water.
Serves 4.

Garlic Prawns with
Vegetables

Simmered Whole Fish

1 × 1 kg whole fish
6 cups water
2 shallots, cut into large
   pieces
2 thin slices, fresh green
   ginger, finely chopped
2 tablespoons sherry
1 tablespoon soy sauce
2 tablespoons oil
4 shallots, sliced finely

2 slices red ginger, finely
   sliced
2 tablespoons soy sauce
2 extra tablespoons oil
1 teaspoon sesame oil

Clean and scale fish, leaving head and tail on. Score, rinse under cold running water and drain.

Bring water to the boil. Add shallots, ginger, sherry, salt and oil to the water and return to boil.

Place fish on a skimmer and lower into the boiling liquid. Reduce heat, cover and simmer gently 5 minutes. Turn off heat completely and leave, covered, for 20 to 25 minutes. Remove the fish carefully onto serving platter. Sprinkle over finely sliced shallots, red ginger and soy sauce. Heat extra oil and sesame oil until sizzling, and pour over fish.
Serves 4.

Crab Foo Yung

4 eggs
1 teaspoon soy sauce
½ teaspoon chilli sauce
2 teaspoons sherry
1 cup fresh or canned
   crabmeat
3 tablespoons oil
6 shallots, minced
6 Chinese dried
   mushrooms, soaked and
   sliced

Sauce:
1 cup chicken stock
2 teaspoons soy sauce
1 tablespoon cornflour
blended with
1 tablespoon water

Finely chop crabmeat.

Stir fry vegetables.

Fry omelette mixture in four portions.

Beat the eggs lightly in a bowl. Stir in soy and chilli sauce and sherry. Shred the crabmeat.

Heat 1½ tablespoons oil in wok, stir fry shallots and mushrooms for 2 minutes; add crabmeat and stir fry 1 minute over high heat.

Remove the wok from the heat and cool the mixture a few minutes. Add the egg mixture.

Heat 2 tablespoons of oil in wok. Add a quarter of the mixture and cook the omelette until just set and lightly browned on the underside. Turn and continue cooking for 1 minute. Place omelette on a serving plate. Repeat to make 4 omelettes. Serve with Foo Yung sauce.

To make sauce bring stock, soy sauce and blended cornflour to the boil, stirring constantly. Simmer for 1 minute.

Crab Foo Yung

Deep Fried Whole Fish and Vegetables in Sweet and Sour Sauce

Deep Fried Whole Fish and Vegetables in Sweet and Sour Sauce

1 large whole fish, cleaned and scaled
1 recipe Sweet and Sour Sauce II
2 carrots, sliced diagonally (optional)
2 tablespoons oil
1 clove garlic, crushed
2 thin slices fresh green ginger, grated
1 medium onion, cut into wedges
1 small green pepper, cut into strips
4 fresh mushrooms, sliced
125 g bamboo shoots, shredded

oil for deep frying
1 egg, beaten
cornflour

Bone fish leaving sides attached at tail. Score fish lightly on both sides.

Prepare the Sweet Sour Sauce but do not thicken.

Parboil carrots in water for 4–5 minutes. Cool under cold running water.

Heat 2 tablespoons oil in wok. Add garlic and ginger, stir fry for 1 minute. Discard garlic and ginger. Add onion, pepper, carrots, mushrooms and bamboo shoots and stir fry 2–3 minutes.

Stir in Sweet Sour Sauce, cover and cook for about 1½

minutes. Remove from heat.

Heat oil for deep frying. Brush fish, inside and out, with beaten egg and dredge with cornflour. Deep fry the fish for about 6 minutes or until golden brown and tender. Remove fish with a skimmer and drain on paper towels.

Bring Sweet Sour Sauce to a boil and stir in blended cornflour to thicken. Place fish on a serving dish and pour over sauce.
Serves 4–6.

Deep Fried Sweet and Sour Fish

1 recipe Sweet and Sour Sauce
1 egg
1 egg white
2½ tablespoons cornflour
2 teaspoons soy sauce
1 teaspoon sherry

500 g fish fillets, cut into 2 cm cubes
Flour
Oil for deep frying

Prepare Sweet Sour Sauce. Mix egg, egg white, cornflour and sherry until smooth. Dredge fish lightly in flour and lightly coat with batter. Heat the oil for deep frying. Add fish cubes, one at a time in

several batches. Deep fry until golden brown.

Remove and drain. Transfer to a serving dish. Pour hot Sweet Sour Sauce over and serve.
Serves 4.

Chinese tea

ENTERTAINING

CHINESE entertain in style with great care in the presentation of each dish. Usually more expensive ingredients are chosen and these are included in dishes which require more skilful preparation. Decorations and garnishes are very important making each dish a visual delight as well as an eating pleasure.

When planning a Chinese meal for entertaining, choose dishes that are cooked in a variety of ways. It is advisable not to choose all stir-fried dishes as you will be constantly in the kitchen cooking the dinner, not entertaining! Most Chinese dishes are suitable for entertaining, however the specialised banquet dishes usually require more expensive ingredients and can be time-consuming to prepare.

The classical accompaniments to Chinese food are tea and wine. Tea is drunk before and after the meal; and wine with the meal.

Chinese tea is drunk for its subtle qualities of taste and fragrance. Sugar, milk or lemon are never added because any of these additions would ruin its bouquet.

Though there are many varieties of tea, there is an accepted classification which divides all of the teas into three groups according to the way in which they are processed. These groups are green tea, black tea and oolong. For green tea, the top leaves are harvested and dried in the sun or in a drying house. This process results in leaves of a dull grayish green colour and produces a pale lightly coloured brew.

Black tea is made from leaves which are not harvested until they are withered. The leaves are then subjected to a process of rolling and fermenting before they are dried. Black tea produces a reddish brown brew.

With the oolong type of tea, the fermentation or oxidizing is stopped halfway and the leaves are only partly dried. The brew produced is rich and golden amber in colour. In China, teas are often scented with dried blossoms which are added to the leaves. Jasmine tea is a well known example.

When brewing green tea, use one teaspoon of tea for every four cups of water to start with, and regulate the amount of tea to your own taste the next time. For black tea, use one teaspoon of tea, or slightly less, for every cup of water. Follow the usual method for making tea: warmed pot and freshly boiled water.

Soy Coloured Eggs

4 eggs
½ cup soy sauce
½ cup chicken stock or water
½ cup sugar
¼ teaspoon sesame oil
1 tablespoon grated onion
4 radishes, sliced
plum sauce or hoisin sauce

Place the eggs in a saucepan. Cover with cold water and boil gently for 5 minutes. Remove from the heat and stand under cold running water for 5 minutes. Remove the shells carefully under cold water.

Place the soy sauce, chicken stock, sugar, sesame oil and onion in a small saucepan. Bring the mixture to boiling point. Add the eggs, cover the pan and simmer for 10 minutes.

Remove from the heat and allow the eggs to cool in the sauce for 30 minutes. Turn the eggs during the cooking and cooling to ensure that they are coloured evenly.

Drain the eggs and cut into quarters lengthwise. Serve with radishes and plum or hoisin sauce. These eggs may be served either as part of a meal or cold as an appetizer. Serves 4.

Marbled Tea Eggs

4 eggs
3 cups boiling water
2 tablespoons tea leaves
1 teaspoon salt
2 cloves star anise

Place the eggs in a pan and cover with cold water. Bring to a boil. Reduce heat and simmer 5 minutes. Remove, drain and run cold water over them for several minutes. Dry the eggs and tap the shells gently with back of spoon on all sides to crack them evenly.

Place the 3 cups boiling water in a saucepan with the tea, salt and star anise. Add the eggs, cover and simmer gently for 1½ hours.

Let the eggs cool in the flavoured water ½ hour. The eggs may be made in advance but do not shell them until ready to serve. Shell under cold water.

Serve halved or quartered as an appetizer. Serves 4.

Dim Sims

500 g green prawns
¼ teaspoon sesame oil
1 egg white
2 teaspoons sugar
1 tablespoon soy sauce
2 shallots, finely chopped
8 dried Chinese
  mushrooms, soaked and
  chopped
6 water chestnuts, finely
  chopped
125 g wonton skins

Finely chop prawns and stir in combined sesame oil, egg white, sugar and soy sauce. Mix in shallots, mushrooms and water chestnuts.

Brush wonton skin lightly with water. Using the left hand, hold thumb and index finger in a circle. Cover the circle with one wonton wrapper. Top with a teaspoonful of filling. Using teaspoon, press and push the filling and wrapper through the circle to form a drawstring pouch. Close finger and thumb together to produce a draw string effect.

Steam for 20 minutes on a base of green vegetables. To do this, bring 5 cm of water to boil in a wok and line a steamer with outside lettuce leaves. Place dim sims on top, allowing space between each one. Place steamer in wok, cover, and steam above boiling water for 20 minutes. Remove and serve with a dipping sauce (see Dipping Sauce recipe).
Note: Make sure there is some boiling water at hand in case water in wok needs to be topped up.

Sang Choy Bow (Pork and Lettuce Rolls)

30 g dried Chinese
  mushrooms
45 g water chestnuts
60 g bamboo shoots
3 shallots
1 small can crab
2 teaspoons oil
125 g minced pork
1 teaspoon sesame oil
2 teaspoons soy sauce
1 teaspoon oyster sauce
1 tablespoon sherry
1 lettuce, washed and
  dried

Cover mushrooms with very hot water and stand 20 minutes, drain, remove stems and chop mushroom caps finely. Very finely chop water chestnuts, bamboo shoots and shallots. Drain and flake crab.

Heat oil in wok and stir fry pork until golden. Stir in mushrooms, water chestnuts, bamboo shoots, shallots and crab. Cook 1 minute. Combine sesame oil, soy sauce, oyster sauce and sherry and stir into the mixture. Place 2 level tablespoons of the mixture into the centre of each lettuce leaf. Fold in the ends of the lettuce leaf and roll up to form a neat parcel.

Generally, meat filling and lettuce leaves are served separately, guests fill and roll their own lettuce leaves.

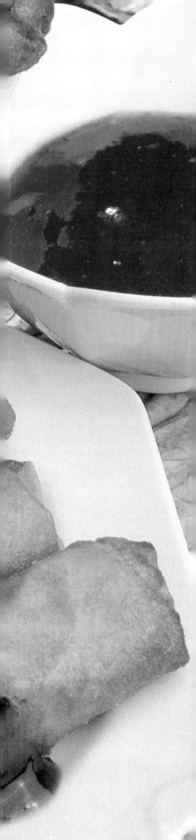

Spring Rolls

8 spring roll wrappers
1 onion, finely chopped
1 tablespoon oil
125 g lean ham, diced
125 g bean sprouts
1 teaspoon soy sauce
oil for deep frying

Alternative Filling:
125 g minced pork
2 teaspoons soy sauce
1 tablespoon oil
4 Chinese dried
 mushrooms, soaked and
 sliced
60 g Chinese cabbage,
 shredded
125 g water chestnuts

Stir soy sauce into ham and vegetables.

Place filling on one side of wrapper.

Fold over short side and tuck underneath.

Fold in both ends of wrapper.

Roll up, dampening remaining corner before pressing firmly to the roll.

Deep fry rolls and allow to drain.

Heat oil in wok and stir fry onions until clear. Add ham and bean sprouts, stir fry gently for 1½ minutes. Stir soy sauce through mixture. Allow to cool.
　　Spoon 2 tablespoons ham and onion filling on to each spring roll wrapper, fold over at ends and roll up, pressing edges in firmly. Stand for 15 minutes.
　　Heat oil in wok. Deep dry spring rolls until golden. Serve hot with dipping sauce. Serves 4.

Note: To cook alternative filling: season pork with soy sauce. Heat oil in wok and stir fry. Stir in the mushrooms and cabbage and cook for 4 minutes. Stir in the water chestnuts.

Festive Noodles

1 teaspoon salt
350 g egg noodles
2 tablespoons oil
1 onion, diced finely
¼ white cabbage,
 shredded
250 g boned chicken
 breast, cut into strips

3 fresh chillies, finely
 chopped
2 teaspoons soy sauce
1 teaspoon sesame oil
oil for deep frying

Heat water to boiling, add salt and noodles and bring to boil. Cook for 5–6 minutes until tender. Drain and set aside to cool and dry.
　　Heat oil in wok and stir fry onion, cabbage, chicken and chillies till tender. Stir through soy sauce and set

aside. Keep warm.
　　Heat oil for deep frying. Plunge noodles into oil inside strainer. Fry until crisp. Remove with strainer. Place on serving dish with chicken in centre.
Serves 4.

Spicy King Prawns

1 kg prawns
¼ cup oil
2 cloves garlic, crushed
2 fresh chillies, chopped
 finely
1 teaspoon chilli sauce
1 tablespoon soy sauce

2 tablespoons tomato
 sauce
2 teaspoons cornflour
blended with
2 tablespoons water
2 cups fried rice
1 cup bean sprouts

Peel prawns, leaving tail intact. Heat oil in wok, add garlic, chillies and prawns and stir fry for 5–6 minutes. Add chilli, soy and tomato sauces. Heat thoroughly and thicken with blended cornflour.

　　Combine fried rice and bean sprouts and serve with prawns.
Serves 4.

Pork Spare Ribs

3 kg pork spare ribs cut
  into 5 cm pieces
⅓ cup clear honey
3 tablespoons soy sauce
1 tablespoon lemon juice
2 teaspoons fresh ginger,
  finely grated

Preheat oven to 190°C (375°F). Place ribs on a rack over 2 cm water in a baking dish. Bake for 45 minutes.

Warm honey, soy sauce, lemon juice and ginger. Remove from heat.

Lower oven temperature to 170°C (325°F). Continually baste the ribs with the honey sauce for 30 minutes, turning ribs occasionally.

Serve with Fried Rice. Serves 6.

Beef with Pepper

500 g rump steak
⅓ cup oil
1 large onion, cut into
  wedges
2 sticks celery, sliced
  diagonally
1 green capsicum, cubed
5 Chinese dried

mushrooms, soaked and
  sliced
1 cup stock
3 tablespoons soy sauce
2 teaspoons cornflour
blended with
1 tablespoon stock

Cut meat across the grain into thin strips. Heat oil in wok and stir fry beef in batches for 4–5 minutes. Remove and set aside. Stir fry onion, celery and capsicum 3–4 minutes. Add mushrooms and stir fry 30 seconds.

Return meat, add stock and soy sauce, bring to the boil. Thicken with blended cornflour.
Serves 4.

Deep Fried Pork Balls

750 g minced pork
½ teaspoon grated fresh
  green ginger
3 water chestnuts,
  chopped
4 shallots, finely chopped
1 tablespoon soy sauce
2 teaspoons sherry
2 tablespoons cornflour
1 egg

oil for deep frying
shredded lettuce

Combine the minced pork, ginger, water chestnuts and shallots. Mix thoroughly with soy sauce, sherry, cornflour and egg.

Form the mixture into 16 balls.

Heat the oil for deep frying. Fry the balls, in batches, for about 3 minutes.

Remove and drain. Deep fry all the balls together a second time for about 2 minutes until lightly browned and crisp. Drain and serve on a bed of shredded lettuce.

Serve plain or with a Sweet Sour Sauce. Serves 6.

Bamboo Shoots with Pork

500 g lean pork
½ cup soy sauce
1 tablespoon sherry
2 teaspoons cornflour
½ cup oil
125 g bamboo shoots,
  sliced
6 shallots, cut in 2 cm
  pieces

Slice the pork across the grain then cut into 4 cm pieces. Combine with 2 tablespoons soy sauce, sherry and cornflour. Heat oil in wok. Add pork and stir fry, in batches, until the meat

changes colour. Remove and keep warm. Add the bamboo shoots, remaining soy sauce and sugar.

Lower heat and simmer for 5 minutes, stirring occasionally. Return the pork

and heat through. Add shallots and stir fry 1 minute. Serve with egg noodles or Chinese Rice.
Serves 4.

Fortune Cookies, Moon Cookies and fresh fru

DESSERTS

THE Chinese very rarely eat desserts and most are reserved for banquets, formal dinners or are made for one of the many festivals that the Chinese celebrate.

Fresh fruit in season is a good choice for people who like to finish a meal with something sweet. Fortune cookies are always baked commercially and are available, in packets, from Chinese speciality shops. Moon cakes, which are also available from shops, are never prepared at home as they are time consuming and require a long list of unusual ingredients. The cakes are filled with a lightly sweetened, rich-red soybean paste and are exchanged as gifts at the Moon Festival, during September.

Fruit ices would be another suitable dessert for a Chinese meal. Marco Polo was introduced to these on his voyage to China and brought the idea back to the Western world.

Peking Dust

1 large can unsweetened chestnut puree
¼ cup sugar
2 cups cream
3 tablespoons caster sugar
1 teaspoon vanilla essence
1 tablespoon brown sugar
½ cup sugar
¼ cup water
1 small can mandarin orange segments
60 g almonds, blanched

Whip cream, caster sugar and vanilla, beating until stiff. Divide into 2 equal portions. Fold brown sugar and chestnut puree into one portion of the cream until well blended. Fill a lightly oiled bowl with the chestnut mixture and press down firmly. Invert the chestnut cream onto a plate and top with the remaining cream.

Dissolve the sugar in the water over gentle heat then boil for 5 minutes. Dip the fruits and nuts into the syrup. Cool and harden on a greased surface. Decorate the Peking Dust with the fruits and nuts.

Serves 6–8.
Note: When fresh chestnuts are available, substitute 1 kg fresh for the canned and prepare as follows: Score chestnuts crosswise on the flat side. Place on an oven tray and roast in a 200°C (400°F) oven for about 15 minutes or until slightly opened. Cool and skin. Place chestnuts in a wok and cover with water. Bring to boil and cook for about 25 minutes or until just tender. Puree and combine with the ¼ cup sugar. Sweeten to taste.

Toffee Apples

4 ripe apples
1 egg
1 egg white
2 tablespoons flour
2 tablespoons cornflour
Oil for deep frying
¼ cup oil
¼ cup sugar
¼ cup honey
1½ tablespoons white sesame seeds (optional)
1 bowl of iced water

Dip apple wedges in batter.

Deep fry until crisp and golden.

Coat fritters with syrup and sprinkle with sesame seeds.

Peel and core the apples and cut each apple in 6 to 8 wedges. Beat the egg and egg white together and fold in sifted flour and cornflour.

Heat the oil for deep frying. Dip apple wedges in the batter and deep fry until golden. Remove and drain on paper towels.

In a saucepan heat the ¼ cup oil, add sugar and heat, stirring constantly, until the sugar has dissolved. Stir in the honey.

Coat fritters with syrup and sprinkle with sesame seeds.

Serve while piping hot. Let each guest dip the apple fritters into the ice water. This will cause the syrup coating to harden so that the fritters will be crisp and crackling on the outside.
Serves 4.
Note: The Toffee Apples can be pre-prepared up to the stage of dipping in the syrup. At this stage everything should be ready. For your first try, test on the family so you can get the timing correct.

Toffee Appl●

Eight Precious Pudding

2 cups long grain rice
250 g assorted dried and
  glacé fruits and nuts
4 cups water
¼ cup sugar
6 tablespoons lard
⅔ cup red bean paste
1 cup water
⅔ cup sugar
1 teaspoon almond
  essence
1 tablespoon cornflour
3 tablespoons cold water

Wash rice and drain. Prepare fruit and nuts (see note below).

Place rice in a wok, add 4 cups water and bring to boil. Reduce heat, cover and cook over low heat about 25 minutes or until dry and fluffy. Cool slightly and add ¼ cup sugar and 4 tablespoons lard. Grease a heatproof bowl or dish generously with remaining melted lard. Allow to cool. Arrange fruits and nuts in an attractive pattern over base and sides of bowl pressing lightly into the lard.

Carefully fill bowl with half the rice, pressing gently. Spread with a layer of bean paste, keeping within 3 to 4 cm of sides. Add remaining rice and press down gently so the pudding will hold its shape when it is unmoulded.

Cover with greased foil and steam 1 hour. Remove bowl from steaming pan and invert pudding onto serving plate. Heat 1 cup water, sugar and almond essence until sugar has dissolved. Bring to boil. Blend cornflour with water. Add to boiling syrup and stir until thickened. Pour sauce over pudding and serve hot or cold.
Serves 8.
Note: The original Chinese recipe prescribes dried or preserved fruits and nuts which are not obtainable in this country. They can be substituted, however, by your choice of dried or glacé fruits, such as prunes, raisins, sultanas, dates, cherries, apricots, orange peel and nuts such as almonds, walnuts, lotus seeds, melon seeds etc. It is best to have at least 8 different items to justify the name of the pudding. Nuts should be blanched and halved. The fruits should be pitted and halved or quartered, if large.

Fruits, especially glacé fruits, can be cut into half moon or other patterns to make an attractive decoration.

Almond Cookies

1 cup sugar
250 g lard
1 egg
1–2 teaspoons almond
  essence
3 cups plain flour
1½ teaspoons baking
  powder
¼ teaspoon salt
¾ cup blanched ground
  almonds
whole blanched almonds
  for decoration

Cream the sugar and lard together until light and fluffy. beat in the egg and almond essence. Sift together flour, baking powder and salt. Add 1 cup of the flour mixture and the ground almonds, combine thoroughly. Add the remaining flour.

Knead the dough until smooth. Roll to 6 mm thickness on a floured board. Cut the cookies with a 4 cm round or fluted cutter.

Transfer to a greased oven tray. Place a whole almond in the centre of each cookie. Bake in a preheated moderate oven (180°C/350°F) for 20 minutes or until light brown. Cool on wire racks. Makes approximately 30.

Almond Cookies

ght Precious Pudding

Deep Fried Ice-Cream Balls

1 litre vanilla ice-cream
plain flour
2 eggs, lightly beaten
2 tablespoons water
½ packet 'Nice' (or
  similar) biscuits, crushed
oil for deep frying

Turn the freezer to the coldest setting. Place two baking trays in the freezer.

Quickly scoop out ice-cream balls from the ice-cream using a scoop or a tablespoon. Quickly place the ice-cream on the baking trays and return to the freezer for at least two hours.

Place the flour in a dish, beat the eggs and water in another dish and place the biscuit crumbs in another dish.

Working very quickly, dip the ice-cream balls in the flour then the egg and finally the crumbs. Place on the baking trays and return to the freezer. Leave in the freezer for at least two hours. (At this stage, the ice-cream can be frozen for up to two months). When ready to serve, heat oil for deep frying. Fry the balls, two at a time, until golden brown. Remove immediately and serve with a chocolate or caramel sauce.
Serves 4.

Watermelon and Lychees

This recipe is included for all those who love the combination of lychees and watermelon. Although not traditional, many Chinese restaurants offer this as a dessert.

1 watermelon
1 can lychees in syrup

Cut away the top one-third of the melon.

Scoop out the fruit with the melon ball scoop, making neat round balls. Carefully remove any seeds.

Combine the melon balls and lychees with their syrup.

Place the combined fruits in a serving dish and chill for 1 hour before serving.
Serves 6.

Note: When fresh lychees are in season use these. Simply peel the fruit and use whole. Warn people about the seed.

Almond Float

2½ cups milk
¼ cup sugar
almond essence to taste
1½ tablespoons gelatine
½ cup water
selection of fresh fruit,
  prepared
1 medium can lychees

Scald the milk, remove from heat and add the sugar. Cool slightly then add the almond essence. Cool. Meanwhile, sprinkle the gelatine over the water and leave until the water is absorbed. Dissolve the gelatine over hot water and cool. Stir into the milk mixture.

When ready to serve, cut the almond gelatine into diamond shapes. Place the fruit in a serving bowl. Place the diamonds on top and serve.
Serves 4.

Almond Float

Index